"Amazing encouragement from the heart of the battle! Chris Plekenpol turns the challenges of war into doorways through which we can experience and know more of Christ in our daily lives. Though the book is designed as a devotional tool to be read day by day, I doubt you're going to be able to put it down."

LOUIE GIGLIO
PASSION CONFERENCES

"Beliefs and values are merely words until tested. Chris Plekenpol is a young man whose beliefs and values have been tested like few men I know. There is no theory here. Just the battle-tested insights of a soldier who has learned to trust his heavenly Father in the valley of the shadow of death. You are going to love this book."

ANDY STANLEY
SENIOR PASTOR, NORTH POINT MINISTRIES

"Faith forged in the crucible of combat! Chris Plekenpol is a warrior, and he has compiled a great guide for victory in battles that we all face."

OLIVER L. NORTH
HOST OF "WAR STORIES" ON FOX NEWS
AND AUTHOR OF THE ASSASSIN

FAITH
IN THE
FOG OF
WAR

CPT CHRIS PLEKENPOL

Multnomah® Publishers *Sisters, Oregon*

FAITH IN THE FOG OF WAR
published by Multnomah Publishers, Inc.

© 2006 by Chris Plekenpol
International Standard Book Number: 1-59052-741-0

Cover design by Studiogearbox.com
Cover image by David Turnley/Corbis

Unless otherwise indicated, Scripture quotations are from:
The Holy Bible, New International Version (NIV) © 1973, 1984 by
International Bible Society used by permission.
The Message by Eugene H. Peterson
©1993, 1994, 1995, 1996, 2000, 2001, 2002
Used by permission of NavPress Publishing Group

For information:
MULTNOMAH PUBLISHERS, INC.
601 N. LARCH ST.
SISTERS, OREGON 97759

Library of Congress Cataloging-in-Publication Data
Plekenpol, Chris.
Faith in the fog of war / Chris Plekenpol.
    p. cm.
    ISBN 1-59052-741-0
    1. Plekenpol, Chris. 2. Soldiers—Religious life. 3. Iraq War,
2003—Personal narratives, American. 4. War—Religious
aspects—Christianity. I. Title.
    BV4588.P54 2006
    956.7044'342'092—dc22
                                        2006009094

06 07 08 09 10—10 9 8 7 6 5 4 3 2 1 0

Contents

Acknowledgments

The biggest thank-you goes to Jesus Christ, who authored my heart. I am so amazed by His grace. The thing with God is, He takes the normal people and allows them do God-sized things by giving them His faith. What a great deal that is. I am just along for the ride. Thank You, Heavenly Father!

Next, I want to thank my mom. She has been a rock for me over the years in every sort of crazy situation that I have found myself in. She is still the prettiest woman I know, and I am so glad to be her son. My mom and I are also the best dance partners you have ever seen. Mom, I can't wait to get home and dance with you. We will rock. I love you, Mom!

I want to thank my dad for putting in the countless hours of contacting people and figuring out how this whole book operation works. My dad is great because he really thinks I can do anything. I come up with the craziest ideas and then somehow we are able to do it. That is fun, and that is what dad's are supposed to do. Empower their kids to fulfill their dreams. This book has really brought us closer and I am so thankful for this opportunity to do this with him. Thanks, Dad!

Next, of course, a big thanks goes to Chris Roberts. This guy has done yeomen's work reading every devotional. Including like 150 that are not in this book. That is dedication! Thank you Chris Roberts!

To Caroline Nash, big thanks to you, who not only went through every word with me on the book, but were also a rock of inspiration while I was in Iraq. You have truly lived out what it is to be a friend. I can't wait to do another book with you. You rock, K-Nash.

To Jacob and Emily Davis, I am so grateful for your friendship and support during my time in combat. There were times when I was definitely wondering how much more I could endure and you were always there.

To Adam Schopper, you put your heart where your mouth was and I appreciate that. You really gave me your all through this season of life. Thank you.

To Brad Weston, for your unwavering support and technical love as we tried for hours and hours to get a good internet connection for Passion and for 7:22. Oh, and your friendship isn't too shabby either.

To Brian Smith, whose tireless efforts and professional editing took this book to the next level. Thank you for working so hard!

To Penny Whipps, thank you so much for your nonstop support. Ever since we met, you have pushed me to do more for Christ and make a difference. I love that and can't say thanks enough. You have become a great and dear friend.

To Andy Stanley, I want to thank you for your teaching and your heart. The men of Apache Company know you from the infinite DVDs and CDs you sent. Oh, and I really appreciate you giving this book to Don Jacobson to get published by Multnomah.

To Louie Giglio, thank you for your inspirational teaching and dedication to my men. We have become friends over this time in Korea and in Iraq. Very rarely do people of great stature lean down to befriend those they do not even know. However, Louie, you have a heart that is deeper than the average man and a laser focus on living your life for Christ. Your impact on my life has been incredible. Thanks, Louie.

Prologue

Iraq. My "home" for the present. The place where I'm writing this book.

It's February 2005. The Iraqi national elections have passed, and we are witnessing the dawning of democracy in a country that has, for the past fifty years, been caught in the quagmire of dictatorship. Freedom has been granted. But still we must battle pockets of resistance along Highway 10, the main route between Ramadi, Fallujah, and Baghdad.

I have trained hard to be where I am in my career. I graduated from the United States Military Academy at West Point. If only I had worked half as zealously on my relationship with God. While I was at West Point, I limited myself to what I call a "fan" relationship with God. I would go to the games on Sunday and talk about Him with the boys, but I didn't really know Him. It wasn't until December 5, 1999, that I gave myself wholly to Him at Southeast Christian Church in Louisville, Kentucky. Since that time, I have lived every day with unbridled passion for Christ.

After I left West Point, the Army put me through Ranger School, Airborne School, Air Assault School, Jumpmaster School, and Special Forces Assessment and Selection. I passed them all. It was not my intent to stay in the Army long enough to end up at war in Iraq, but that is what happened. Now I see that it has all been for God's glory. Still is.

I love what I do. In his book *Wild at Heart*, John Eldredge describes the Warrior Poet. That's how I see myself. We've been trained to think of the Christian man as a "nice guy," tame, unwilling to rock the boat. But Exodus 15:3 says that "the Lord is a warrior." When I read that, I get the sense that He's not afraid to rock the boat at times, and He expects us to fight and rock right there beside Him.

A warrior seeks out the harder right over the easier wrong. He is not faint of heart. These codes were impressed upon me throughout training at West Point and Ranger School and, of course, by my mom. I was taught that honor is defined not by niceness, but by doing what is right. The Warrior Poet is characterized by all that it is untamed, strong, and fearless. He never compromises God's righteousness, but he also embraces the softer side of love.

As a Warrior Poet, I command men ready for battle. I never used to think of myself as a Warrior Poet, but I always dreamed of becoming one. I entertained aspirations of living fearlessly in the face of death. But I was afraid. Afraid I could not do it.

I found out I can. I'm doing it now. It's as if I were dropped into the ocean and given two options—sink or swim. Of course, my desire was to swim. But without my God watching over me, I'd be out of my depth, even with all of my training and conditioning. That's why I cling to Him like a little girl to her father's leg. It's good that this task is an impossible one—one that involves pain and struggle. If I didn't need God, I wouldn't seek and find new strength of character in Him. I have learned this while walking the hard road that has led me here, to my sixth month in Iraq. As you read this, I may still be here fighting, or I may already have departed this earth to enjoy Glory forever. None of us knows what tomorrow may bring.

I am not so different from you. Before my deployment to Iraq, the Army was just a job. It was a place to go and work, and then I came home. I never thought of myself as a noble hero. But September 11, 2001, put everything into new perspective. For the first time, I felt that I was part of a Warrior Class. I left the 82nd Airborne Division and, after further captain-schooling and a year in Korea, found myself deployed as a company commander here in Iraq in the summer of 2004.

Before Iraq, I had never seen a real dead person. But within a month of my arrival, I was searching the highway for one of my soldiers. When I found him, I could not even recognize the playful, funny, crazy kid who had only hours before joked about being, in truth, a Delta Force Operative working undercover as a loader in my tank company. I have watched the enemy die and wondered in my heart if it was wrong to witness a man in the moment of his final heartbeat and be glad. I have picked up our own dead more times than I want to remember, questioning secretly why, when I said, "In the name of Jesus, get up and walk," nothing happened.

I prayed desperately for a lieutenant who lay dying in the arms of one of my medics. He had decided to come out into sector because he didn't feel involved. As he crossed over from earth to eternity, I had to tell his best friend, "Keep it together! You have men to lead! Wipe your eyes, and let's go!" when the whole time I just wanted to sit down and cry.

I have spoken at two memorials and shed tears at ten others. I have prayed with my men, wept with my men, bled with my men. In all this, my goal and my heart's cry has been to see God glorified somehow in this surreal world that reminds me of hell more than it does the birthplace of civilization.

I have lived through firefights, bullets flying at me, my bullets flying back. I have kicked in doors, like they do in the movies, the jamb splintering and the door falling at my feet. I have arrested more men than I can remember. I have cuffed them and blindfolded them and taken them away. I have watched women beat themselves in confusion, trying to fathom the reality that I'm taking away their only source of income. I have felt the steel grip of an old woman trying to make me understand why I should not take her son. I have removed my sunglasses for her, so she could see I have a heart, that I am not some sort of soulless, faceless robot.

I have hugged kids and given them soccer balls and Beanie Babies. It made their entire year. I have taken away their fathers. It was their worst nightmare. Many times I have wanted to emotionally detach myself from these people. But that would be a kind of death. I choose to live.

I have written this book so that you might step into my world for a moment and see this life through my eyes. I constantly struggle to "work out my salvation with fear and trembling." I know I'm heaven-bound, but I also realize that I have a lot to "work out" in order to know God better and to plumb the depths of His heart.

I love God with everything that I am. And, being human, I fall short daily in my efforts to live out my thanks to Jesus Christ. See? I told you that you and I are a lot alike. I'm here, not because I'm braver or bolder, but simply because God chose to put me here, and not somewhere else. At heart, each of us is that Warrior Poet that God is calling to step up, to claim our rightful place as heirs to His throne. We are the children of God! And each day of my life is a new lesson about what that means.

What you are about to read is a compilation of e-mails I wrote from Iraq to those who were concerned, to those who were praying, to those who were learning what it was to follow after God. In my writings, I've described events I have experienced and witnessed in Iraq. And I have told it the way it happened, sometimes on the very day it happened. I believe God had a purpose in shaping into a book my firsthand account of war and my relationship with Him, and I'm excited to learn how He will use it. I pray that as you read this, you will be challenged to relentlessly pursue His purpose for you. That you will live out loud for the cause of Christ.

The Calm Before the Storm

CAMP CASEY, KOREA, JUNE 2004

The tempest seen off to the west,
This day shall bring my greatest test.
With knuckles white I gasp for breath,
Sweat trickles down. I think of death.
Heightened fear begins to form.
It is the calm before the storm.

All alone I pace about
Trying to control my doubt.
"Will I be okay? Will I know what to do?"
These thoughts I need the answer to.
I glance to heaven, but feel far away,
Can't think of the right words to say.
Inside I grieve, my heart has torn.
Agony, this calm before the storm.

If only I'd walked and never stumbled.
If only my heart was truly humbled.
Had I not succumbed to the lust of the flesh,
I might have comfort on this eve of death.
Of all the times to feel far away,
Of all the times, unable to pray.
I want to break through in some fashion or form.
I hate the calm before the storm.

Where do you turn when there's no place to go?
Where to turn for rest for the soul?
In quiet desperation, I grasp toward Him,
Asking for peace beyond this sin.
Begging His presence once again.
Asking for hope when all is forlorn.
Hoping He'll fill
My calm before the storm.

I watch clouds pass, the moon shines bright.
All in me wants to run from this fight.
Silence surrounds me. My heart is alone.
Then these words I hear from a Voice that I know:
"Why do you fret and why do you fear?
Why do I find your sweat and tears here?
Have I not told you in times before,
You are my son whom I cannot ignore.
I have known you since before you were born.
I'm with you now,
In the calm before the storm."

He continues, His voice is silent and clear.
The power of His presence so oppressively near.
"As your Father, I have a secret I want you to know.
Take this with you wherever you go.
Whenever you're faithless, I am faithful,
Even when sin has taken its toll.
For I AM the calm before the storm.
I AM here at the center of this storm."

What a moment before was painful angst,
What before made me lose my heart and my strength,
Is now the source of what draws me close,
Makes clear Whom and what I value most.
Because this storm, as well, shall pass.
And He's the peace that's going to last.
His gifts of joy and pain reveal
A need in me I can't conceal:
I need a Savior, I need a Lord
Who is
The Calm Before the Storm.

Get That Hairdryer Out of My Face!

August 1, 2004

It's 8 p.m. local time. We've just arrived in Kuwait, and the friendly airport people are driving over to us the stairs-on-wheels that help us troopers disembark from the aircraft. My nerves are on edge just a little bit. There is a kind of excitement and fear in my gut that is making me slightly unsettled. However, I know this is the beginning of a great adventure. I look out the west window of the plane and see the moon—huge and seemingly low to the ground. I stare, temporarily forgetting where I am. I'm startled back into the present by a slap of hot air against my face as I step off the plane. I assume at first that it's the jet wash of the Boeing 747 World Airline Aircraft. Then I realize that the engines have been stopped for some time now. The nonstop furnace blowing in my face is the desert wind.

It's hard to imagine anywhere being 102 degrees at night, but I definitely feel like I've just stepped into a little kid's Easy Bake Oven. Ironically, 102 is the low for the day, and, as I will find out in the following days, it's pretty mild. Temperatures in the desert can peak at 150. It's like someone sticking a hair dryer in your face, and you can't find the off-switch.

What can I expect in this big desert? In Korea I was surrounded by lush, green mountains. Now I'm scanning what looks like an endless beach. A beach that goes all the way to the ocean two hundred miles away. Everywhere I look…nothing. The term *godforsaken* comes to mind.

What do the locals think of their harsh environment? I

don't think they're exactly thrilled that they live in a desert, but after centuries they have become accustomed to it. Most of them have seen nothing else. They're surrounded by desert in every direction!

Now, I can understand living in a desert if you have no choice. But one thing I've always wondered about: What was the point of Jesus voluntarily going into the desert to be tempted? And what was Paul's pre-ministry desert sojourn all about? Moses spent forty years in the desert before leading Israel out of Egypt. Then he took them back into the desert for another forty years, before Joshua led them into the Promised Land. What is the big deal about hanging out in the desert? Nothing but scorpions, dead camels, and furnace heat. I don't get it.

Then a realization hits me. I pace about, letting the sand slide beneath my boots, and it becomes quite apparent that there are no distractions here. Existence is reduced to the basics. Sure, absorbing the sun's heat in quantities that would power about a million solar-powered calculators for a billion years takes some getting used to. But after you are done whining, and if you happen to be at all inclined toward the spiritual, you have all the time in the world to gain the proper perspective on God. What is the proper perspective? It's this: He is everything and I am nothing. The desert sucks all pride out of you. It shows you your own need. It deepens your character, broadens your awareness, so that you begin to see the needs of others.

This is what Peter was saying when he wrote 1 Peter 4:1–3 to encourage Christians: "Therefore, since Christ suffered in his body, arm yourselves also with the same attitude, because he who has suffered in his body is done with sin. As a result, he does not live the rest of his earthly life for evil human desires, but rather for the will of God. For you have spent enough time in the past doing what pagans choose to do—living in debauchery, lust, drunkenness, orgies, carousing and detestable idolatry." The desert exercised a powerful influence in the lives of our spiritual forefathers Paul and Moses. It burned away who they had been and reshaped and solidified them into who God wanted them to be.

The desert functions the same way in our lives.

I don't know where you are. Maybe in a desert, feeling as though someone is blasting you in the face with a hairdryer. Maybe you have trouble understanding why you are here or how you are to cope. But God lives in the desert with you. Maybe He's using this situation to suck the pride out of you. It could be His time to show you that you are nothing apart from Him. The danger, of course, is that you might forget the refreshing love and forgiveness of God. The Kuwaitis here have no idea what a cool spring breeze coming up from a lush valley feels like. You may have forgotten what it was to live for the will of God. Maybe you've quit trying. You may only remember your sinfulness.

Or maybe you're living the wonderful Christian life and you're totally comfortable with it. You've never struggled through any real trials, and you're quick to judge others who are struggling. Since you have not experienced need, you have not experienced depth. If that's you, I challenge you to put yourself in a position where God becomes an obvious necessity. Step out of the kiddie-pool and go dive into the deep end of the grownup pool.

Are you in the desert? Is your heart wandering around in the furnace, searching for an oasis? For rest? Do you have pride that needs to be purified out? Have you been operating on Christian Cruise Control with no real challenges in your life? Has the ease of your existence left you a spiritually shallow person? What needs to change?

Remember: "God opposes the proud but gives grace to the humble" (James 4:6; see also 1 Peter 5:5 and Proverbs 3:34).

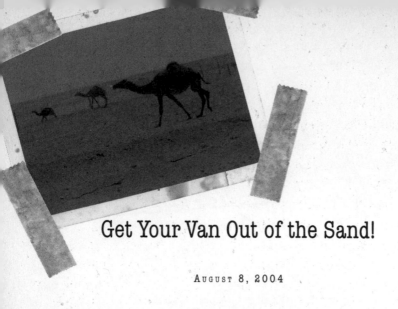

Get Your Van Out of the Sand!

AUGUST 8, 2004

I saw my first camels today. We were getting in some tank target practice. On the way back from holding a reconnaissance of the marksmanship ranges that I would conduct with my men, I saw one of the most interesting spectacles I have ever witnessed. You look around at a vast wasteland of sand, and there in the middle of it are these huge beasts hanging out, eating scrub brush. They come in many different colors; I saw black, brown, and white. Who would have thought? A white camel. I felt as if I had been transplanted back into biblical times. That is, until a pickup truck drove onto the scene and started herding them.

I was in a minivan, in a small convoy of minivans with the other senior-ranking officers of the battalion and we were driving through the desert. Now, when I say "through the desert," I really mean *through the desert*. You don't find many paved roads out here. Or, for that matter, much of anything that resembles what we consider to be civilization.

Driving through the desert in a two-wheel-drive, twelve-passenger van, one might assume that we would get stuck in the sand. That assumption would be correct. Camels do well on sand; they're made for the desert. Minivans aren't and don't.

When we got stuck, I instantly pictured my driver and myself crawling across the dunes, panting for water. However, the convoy of vehicles with which I was traveling stopped and turned around. Everyone got out in the 120-degree heat and started pushing on the rear of the van. After several minutes of toil and a whole day's worth of profanity, we got the van out of the sand and onto a patch of rocky ground where I remounted and proceeded back to the base camp.

On this particular convoy, the colonel, the majors, and the other commanders had come along. Every one of us got out and pushed with everything we had. It was a true bonding moment. There is something about misery and cooperative toil that draws people together. The higher-ups could have stayed in their vehicles and watched me struggle, but that would never happen. Out here in the desert we are the only family that each of us has. We really have no choice but to look after one another. So as we walked back to our respective minivans, I had a newfound trust and confidence in the colonel who was leading me in combat, the majors who were responsible for giving everything I needed to succeed in combat, and my fellow company commanders who would be fighting to my left and to my right.

John Mark, the writer of the Gospel we call "Mark," had a relational desert experience. He ventured off with Paul and Barnabas on Paul's first missionary expedition. After their second stop, John Mark flaked out and went back to Jerusalem. He quit. Now, he didn't lose his salvation over this. He remained a member of Christ's family. But John Mark's mistake really hurt Paul. So much so that Paul would not take him on his next journey.

However, one man did reach out to Mark when no one else would. Barnabas. Barnabas knew the young man had potential, and he sought to develop it. (It also helped that Barnabas was John Mark's cousin.) Barnabas got out of his car and started pushing Mark's van out of the sand. His muscles tightened under the weight, but he would not give up. He would not give in. This was family. Not only was Mark a blood relative, Mark was his brother in Christ. Barnabas was going to do whatever it took to restore Mark. This is love. Barnabas could have left John Mark in his struggle in the desert. He could simply have ventured out again with Paul. But he chose to become lesser to make John Mark greater. As a result, Mark became a beacon for the Christian faith and wrote a biography of the Messiah.

As a Christian, you will have desert experiences. You will fall and watch others fall. You will struggle, trying to push your van out of the sand, hoping that someone will come alongside to push with you. But too many times we as Christians shoot our wounded, rather than meeting them in the midst of their need. We see our Christian brothers and sisters struggling, and we drop them from our lives. Too much trouble, too much heartache. They are "unreliable." They are "not real Christians."

Maybe you've done the wounding. Maybe you are the wounded one. Maybe you've quit.

Whatever the situation, Christ never wants us to grow weary in doing good (Galatians 6:9). Especially for each other.

When was a time you dropped someone because they were wounded? When was a time someone dropped you? Did you quit? Do you look the other way when someone that you feel has "flaked out" wants to reenter the race for Christ? Are you able to love those who have let you down? How would Jesus handle that? In what way are you getting out of the car and helping push someone's van out of the sand?

Remember: We are already set apart in this world. Let us reach down and lift our brothers and sisters up.

Wiccans Will Wonder

August 11, 2004

Last night was amazing. It was the first night of Apache Prayer. Apache Prayer is a time when I gather all those who want to call upon the name of the Lord for guidance, protection, and hope. In light of the hostilities in Najaf and our upcoming entrance into Iraq, tensions are running a bit high. I was tired, but had decided in my heart that prayer was what my company needed above all. I recruited my new driver, SGT Oates, to make the rounds for a call to prayer. There were only three of us—First SGT Sartin, SGT Oates, and myself. I wrote down their prayer requests, and we went to the throne of grace. I prayed for the Spirit of God to enter the hearts of all my men. I prayed that His glory would be shown through all we do, and that we would have the wisdom to make the right decisions. I prayed that the fear of the unknown that lay only a week or so away would be comforted by His grace. Most importantly, I prayed that we would hear the voice of God and obey.

Now, you must realize that I am in a tent with sixty other men, so what we do, we do in public. One soldier, in particular, gets irritated every time I talk about God, as if I were imposing religion on him. And last night it just so happened that our prayers were in the vicinity of this guy. As we finished praying, he got up and came over to First SGT Sartin and me. We braced ourselves for a confrontation. "I eavesdropped on your praying," he started, "and I was wondering…" We were surprised to find that he had approached us to inquire, not to criticize.

First SGT Sartin and I talked with him for an hour about the gospel. It was incredible. All my fatigue went away as the power and excitement of the gospel injected me—and seemingly everything around me—with new life. This man, who was a Wiccan, had been watching us and could not help seeing "something more" in the lives, and in the prayers, of a few of us.

After conversing with this soldier, I went back to my cot and found a note. It was a prayer to the Lord from another soldier. He had heard us praying and wanted me to send one up for him. He also happened to be a Wiccan. His prayer started, "Lord, I know it has been a long time since we talked, but…" Amazing.

The last two people in the company in whom I thought God's Spirit would spark an interest in Himself were these two. One hated any mention of God. The other felt ripped off by God, and, as a kid, joined the Jehovah's Witnesses, but later became an avid fan of the band Slipknot and anything satanic. How does that happen? How does God take people from the extreme far end of the spectrum and reveal Himself to them?

In large part, it happens because He uses us. When we boldly proclaim the gospel—out of love, not pride—we're fulfilling one of our most important missions on earth. For me, it's easy; I am about to witness people dying, so eternity seems very real to me. In fact, the written prayer of the Slipknot fan was all about death. He prayed that if he died fighting for freedom, he would end up in God's hands and his family would be taken care of.

Why am I here right now? I am here to live and speak boldly for Christ because there are so many souls who need to hear and who need to enter into the kingdom. God is going to use me.

In the midst of persecution in Jerusalem, Peter and John spoke openly about the Lord to their people, the Jews. They were imprisoned. Upon their release, they launched back into their task with new vigor. And, as they did, they prayed. They praised God for His absolute sovereignty over the world's leaders. Then, concerning those who murdered Jesus and opposed His followers, they affirmed, "They did what your power and will had decided beforehand should happen. Now, Lord, consider their threats and enable your servants to speak your word with great boldness. Stretch out your hand to heal and perform miraculous signs and wonders through the name of your holy servant Jesus" (Acts 4:28–30).

When we pray, we say amen, then go back to mowing the lawn. But according to verse 31, "After they prayed, the place where they were meeting was shaken. And they were all filled with the Holy Spirit and spoke the word of God boldly."

In the middle of the last sentence, I took a break and presented the gospel to the Wiccan who wrote the prayer. What a gift! I can't explain to you the joy of spreading life while living on the verge of death.

For someone in the States or somewhere else out of harm's way, you may be thinking, *How in the world can I apply that? You are in a war zone where people think about death. You have ready-made open doors, but I don't have that luxury.* My answer: Just be bold where you are. Pray for the opportunity to speak, and don't shy away from people who need to hear the gospel.

Jesus said, "I tell you, open your eyes and look at the fields! They are ripe for harvest. Even now the reaper draws his wages, even now he harvests the crop for eternal life, so that the sower and the reaper may be glad together" (John 4:35–36).

Are you living and speaking boldly? Do you pray with fervor for boldness? Do you put yourself in positions where sharing your faith may take its toll on you? Or do you feel like some people are simply out of Christ's reach?

Think again.

Remember: *What is impossible for man is possible with God.*

Poop Trophies

I have traveled the world and lived in many different climates. And everywhere I've gone, I've discovered one constant: From the U.S. to Korea to Kuwait, poop trucks are poop trucks.

We live in tents and use Porta-Potties instead of installed toilets. And when you live this way day in and day out, that wonderful, warm smell permanently permeates your nostrils and makes you want to vomit. Combine that with soldiers whose personal hygiene leaves something to be desired, and you get something I call "fun with poop."

For example, sometimes you step into a Porta-Potty and find a nice present on the toilet seat. Some fastidious trooper, not wanting to touch the seat for fear of germs, hovered in mid-air to drop his cargo. Unfortunately, he missed. And, so, in a radical departure from fastidiousness, he leaves his trophy for all to appreciate.

TMI? (Too much information?) Maybe. But I do have a point. Not many Scripture passages are brought to mind when I see the beauty and smell the aroma of fresh poop on a toilet seat—except for one. It's Philippians 3:7–8, and in it the apostle Paul says, "But whatever was to my profit I now consider loss for the sake of Christ. What is more, I consider everything a loss compared to the surpassing greatness of knowing Christ Jesus my Lord, for whose sake I have lost all things. I consider them rubbish, that I may gain Christ."

A little background. Paul was this guy who was, like, "Rabbi of the year" about five years in a row. He won every religious debate. He was the golden child of the Jewish religious leaders. This guy was amazing! Just before these verses, Paul actually listed his accomplishments. He had received every accolade, punched every ticket, and achieved every success in the eyes of the Jewish world.

But how did Paul feel about his accomplishments? He used a word that the NIV translates as "rubbish" and *The Message* translates as "trash." The "Revised Plekenpol Version" prefers the word "poop." Paul said that's exactly what you get when you rely on your morals or righteous deeds alone.

That's why my efforts end in frustration whenever I try to get by on merely moralistic standards for living. I'm sometimes so proud of the fact that I don't drink. I think of it as "purity," when it really has nothing to do with purity. Some people flaunt the fact that they were a virgin until married, while others tout their amazing church attendance. Some will tell you how God has blessed them with material things. Others will drop names; they'll give you a detailed description of people they know and places they have been. Some love their degrees and prominently display certificates in the office and at home.

All of these are good things. But deeming any of these accomplishments as means to righteousness will always leave us empty. What the world values and what God values are two completely different things. What the world values is temporary; what God values is eternal.

So God sends us a message through Paul: Our accomplishments and merits are trophies—trophies shaped like the poop of the Porta-Potties—sitting on our mantels. There is only one true means of attaining righteousness, and that is by faith, as a gift from God. Since Paul had attained righteousness by this

Mrs. Nina Mascheck

means, he could now live his life serving God. Paul put it like this, "But one thing I do: Forgetting what is behind and straining toward what is ahead, I press on toward the goal to win the prize for which God has called me heavenward in Christ Jesus" (Philippians 3:13–14).

Some of us are still living our lives thinking we can impress God, as though God will somehow love us more for our accomplishments. If God were into accomplishments, then none of us would ever get to heaven. We are incapable of attaining Christlike perfection. What He desires from us is faith. That means we must become broken to a point where we can clearly see how lacking we are and how everything we, on our own, have accomplished in this life is nothing more than human waste. When we have a faith like that, we can move mountains. Then we will be able to see clearly what amazing mission God has prepared us for.

Are you willing to acknowledge that all you have
accomplished cannot make you righteous?
Are you willing to let go of pride and be broken
in spirit before God and man?
Are you ready to be of use to God?

Remember: *"The call of Jesus teaches us that*
our relation to the world has been built on
an illusion" (Dietrich Bonhoeffer, The Cost of
Discipleship).

Need Creates Depth

AUGUST 18, 2004

Yesterday, I led a security detachment to Camp Arifjan in Southern Kuwait. After a long day preparing vehicles and conducting traveling operations, we finished our job and had an hour before we needed to return to Camp Buehring in Northern Kuwait. We decided to go to the mess hall.

Now, if you don't know much about Army mess halls, just know that usually they are drab places where you just want to get your chow and move out. Army chow consists either of some kind of unappetizing meat stew or a conglomeration with vegetables, and that is about it.

Camp Arifjan was ridiculous. The mess hall was like the size of an indoor basketball coliseum. A projector ran a live broadcast of the Olympics from Greece on a twenty-by-forty-foot screen. There was row after row of food. And not just any kind of food. Steak and lobster were the main courses, accompanied by several full salad bars, a small deli with all kinds of cold cuts, and a short-order grill with cheeseburgers, hot dogs, and every kind of greasy, to-die-for food. If that were not enough, the mess hall workers arranged a dessert table that was at least twenty feet long and held every type of cake, from German chocolate to double chocolate.

There were about ten freezers with all the ice cream you could eat. The tables were neatly covered with beautiful table-cloths and ornamentation. The place even had bathrooms with real toilets that flushed! Outside the mess hall was a courtyard that rivaled some malls in the U.S. It boasted such back-home favorites as Subway, Pizza Hut, and Burger King, as well as a dry cleaner, a big PX (department store), and a stage surrounded by bleachers, where someone was going to perform a concert that night.

My compadres and I walked into the mess hall all dirty and smelly, and I noticed that we were the only ones in the joint with weapons. We looked like tourists as we gazed around us, mesmerized. We laughed and held up steak and lobster like they were some great treasure.

As I was eating dinner and guffawing at the bounty before us, I noticed another soldier wearing civilian clothes. His T-shirt read, "Inmate of Camp Arifjan…Release Date: 12-11-04."

I couldn't believe it. How could these people fail to recognize that they were in heaven here? Soldiers had told me they would pick up trash and clean toilets just to be stationed here. The T-shirt made me angry, and I was about to make a scene. But I decided that might not be the best Christian response. But we had come from so little to so much, and here were people who didn't appreciate what they had. They probably have showers where you don't have to turn the water off between soaping and rinsing.

And, of course, this was all free. These soldiers were enjoying the same pay and tax-free status—even hostile-fire pay—all without firing a bullet or ducking the bullet of a hostile enemy.

Standing in Kuwait and letting my mind take me around the world to my own country, I see the same attitude in the U.S. We have so much. Some of our biggest worries revolve around what we are going to wear, not because of a shortage of clothing, but because of the mind-boggling variety. We worry that our car is not cool enough. We worry that we are not pretty enough or skinny enough. We worry that our house is not big enough.

There are Americans who consider themselves inmates of their own world. They'll find freedom and happiness when they can finally escape school. Or their job. Or this stage of life. Or this cruddy marriage.

What a lie.

Paul figured this out. He wrote. "I have learned to be content whatever the circumstances. I know what it is to be in need, and I know what it is to have plenty. I have learned the secret of being content in any and every situation, whether well fed or hungry, whether living in plenty or in want. I can do everything through him who gives me strength." (Philippians 4:11–13)

Most of us cannot honestly echo what Paul wrote: "I know what it is to be in need." Even we Christians shelter ourselves from the rest of the world. We never experience the nonstop hurt and hunger of poverty. We turn our little pains into melodramas that consume us, when we should be giving our hearts fully and selflessly to Christ. We say we want to know God better, but we have no depth. We are not truly broken before God.

The way to create depth is to experience need. Only when we put ourselves in a position to truly experience need will we really begin to appreciate the amazing gift of our country, the awesomeness of God, and realize how badly the world needs to hear the gospel.

When was the last time you really had
to depend on God? Do you live a sheltered life,
but feel like an inmate? Are your eyes open
to the true wealth in your life?
Do you know what real need is?
How can you experience real poverty?
What would it take in order for you to see and
experience need?

Memorize Philippians 4:11–13.

A Soldier Just Can't Say No

AUGUST 28, 2004

Imagine a five-by-five-foot dwelling where a whole family of ten conducts their daily lives. Children sleep on top of each other and wonder every day where their next meal is going to come from. Their gaunt faces and protruding cheekbones only emphasize the hopeless look in their piercing eyes. Hunger is the drive behind their every decision. It is a pang that will never be satisfied. The entire family daily hits the pavement to beg, hoping that a military convoy will take pity on their plight and literally drop crumbs their way.

As we traveled north, our convoy had to stop because of one tractor-trailer's engine problem. As the drivers went to assess the situation and repair the damages, we were greeted by a typical desert family afflicted by extreme poverty. A barefooted, little girl in nothing but a T-shirt pitter-pattered across the blacktop in the 120-degree heat. PVT Murphy saw her puppy-dog eyes and was stricken with compassion. An MRE (meals ready to eat) bag flew in the little girl's direction. She scampered to pick it up and carry it back to her father so that her family could eat.

We are ordered not to give gifts or food to Iraqis because it only encourages more begging, which, in turn, causes little kids to dart between tanks and other vehicles.

However, we are Americans. And when we see need, soldiers can't help but "accidentally" drop a box of food to a beggar. It's just the way we are. We see need, and our hearts fall out.

Some Iraqis will sell everything they have, which is not much, to buy one bottle of liquor. They do it in hopes that an American will buy the liquor, usually for a price that can feed a family for a week.

As the convoy moved north again, I began to think about why American soldiers give so freely. My soldiers, who have no blood ties to these Iraqis, and who have been told not to distribute any food, cannot help but give. Our country has lost one thousand men at this point. There is danger in being nice. A soldier who lets down his guard in any fashion runs the risk of receiving machine-gun fire or may be susceptible to a suicide bomber. In fact, we have sat through class after class about how kids may carry bombs. The enemy knows that Americans are weak when it comes to kids. When an American sees a child, he loves. A soldier's stern face turns to a smile at the sight of a child, and then that soldier will give up everything he has in his vehicle to satisfy the needs of an impoverished young one. The soldier has the ability to meet the need, and the satisfaction of an Iraqi smile is enough reason to act on that ability.

Our heavenly Father responds with the same compassion toward His children. "Which of you, if his son asks for bread, will give him a stone? Or if he asks for a fish, will give him a snake? If you, then, though you are evil, know how to give good gifts to your children, how much more will your Father in heaven give good gifts to those who ask him!" (Matthew 7:9–11).

In the same way a soldier sees a need and meets it, Jesus tells us that our heavenly Father seeks to do the same. We must simply bring our requests to Him. Not because He doesn't know what we need. He simply wants to see the same humility in our eyes that my soldiers see in the eyes of the Iraqi children.

In Luke 11:9–10, Jesus says, "So I say to you: Ask and it will be given to you; seek and you will find; knock and the door will be opened to you. For everyone who asks receives; he who seeks finds; and to him who knocks, the door will be opened."

What are you wanting from God, but not asking for? What dreams are you not pursuing because they are "too big for God"? What do you talk about doing some day, but never ask God to help you with? Stop pining away and be bold before the Father! He can't help giving when His children ask.

The Fog of War

I am finally in the saddle, commanding my company in combat. Combat is one of the most chaotic things ever, especially when you are just starting out. Today was especially ridiculous in that I had the captain, whose company mine was replacing, riding shotgun for me in my tank. I had shadowed him over the past week, trying to learn everything I could. It was like drinking from a fire hose. Now, I am leading men in combat. Such a noble thing. My thoughts of nobleness, however, were erased within the first two minutes of exiting the base. As I approached Khalidiyah, the city that Highway 10 runs through, a Humvee section of infantrymen that had just been attached to me sped across the dirt median and in front of my tank. These two Humvees had no regard for all the training we had been given. We had learned firsthand from the men we were replacing never to cut across the median unless you wanted to hit a roadside bomb. I was furious at my infantrymen and was about to call them on the radio to chew them out, when brown dirt from their wake greeted my face and I was blinded. I told my driver to stop. I did not want to continue through the brownout and hit a civilian or another military vehicle. As we stopped and waited for the dirt to clear, I felt a huge jolt and a loud noise, which, for a moment, I thought was an RPG attack. I ducked down in the turret, and then slowly peered out, expecting a hoard of insurgents to spray down my tank with machine-gun fire. As I looked, I saw what had happened. One of my lieutenants had just barreled into me as he was blinded by the brownout as well. Unbelievable.

"Apache 6, this is White 1, we are going to have to take it in. When we hit you, the seals of the gun tube broke and I don't think we can fire."

Unbelievable. I was not only furious, but very embarrassed. I had the captain of the company I was replacing with me, and I could tell by the look on his face that he thought we were going to be in big trouble. I responded back to my lieutenant. "Roger. Switch out your tank with one of the float tanks."

"This is White 1, roger."

For us, just about everything that could go wrong did go wrong, except, thankfully, that none of my men suffered loss of life or limb.

At the outset of battle, everything seemed to start right. I had prepped my men on the battlefield. We had gone over the significant actions of the last twenty-four hours. I had explained the rules of engagement. I had prayed over everyone. I had made sure that everyone conducted pre-combat inspections. Why, then, had everything fallen apart?

I patrolled the road and offered encouragement back to my command post to "get that other tank out here!" I had four tanks out in sector with six Humvees. Communication with a couple tanks went down, followed by my Humvees that were unable to communicate. Frustration followed embarrassment, and now I was worried that if we were hit, we would be an absolute mess. Without communication, I wouldn't know where all my men were on the battlefield. I prayed through this. I had a flashback to my military science class at West Point. The Prussian military analyst Carl von Clausewitz called this time, "the fog of war." Others call it Murphy's Law. But whatever you want to call it, nothing was going right. And I felt helpless to control it. There was a sense that I felt I had to be everywhere at once. Sure, the commander's presence on the battlefield brought a little clarity, but I could not be everywhere at once. What a commander brings to the battlefield is focus. My men look to me for focus and direction through the fog.

The responsibility of decision-making is taken off the shoulders of the soldier; his responsibility is greatly simplified—he need only do exactly what the commander tells him. Although the situation may seem chaotic, he knows that if he trusts his commander and simply obeys, everything will turn out all right. The commander has the big picture, the training, and the experience to overcome the enemy.

On the battlefield, I bring focus. However, there comes a point where, as a commander, I can feel overwhelmed. And I need direction through the fog of war. I need clarity, and I need God's peace to function so that I may take chaos to calm.

Eventually, another tank made it out to the highway and I headed back in to see if I could better control things from the perspective of a map and some radios. I also wanted to ensure that my communications sergeant was aware of our communications issues. I also wanted to take back the captain who was giving me helpful hints all the way through our first encounters with the highway we will patrol for the next year. As I returned to base, I thought of how I could do this company-commander thing a little better. There just seemed to be so much that I could not control. Overwhelming.

Whether in combat or back in the states, I can be overwhelmed by the enemy. During this time, I must seek Christ's direction to guide me through the fog of war. By trusting Him, I allow him to bring the proper focus to my heart. The spiritual battlefield has its own variety of threats and traumatic experiences. Instead of dealing with RPGs, IEDs, or snipers, you may face the loss of a relationship. Or the loss of a job. You receive blows to your self-image. You wrestle with loneliness.

Many of us start out thinking that Christianity will make everything peachy keen. But that's not really Christianity at all. Christ told us that this life was not going to be easy. The Son of God endured heartache every day. He was tempted in every way. He had to endure loneliness, because no one really understood Him—not even His three closest compadres, Peter, James, and John. He had to endure persecution from religious leaders who could not understand why he hung out with sinners. And then there were the sinners who could not understand why He would hang out with religious leaders. Every day was another chance for Christ to encounter another spiritual ambush. Another temptation.

Yet He was never defeated. His scorecard read: "Jesus ∞, Temptation 0."[2]

I love how Jesus said in John 16:33, "In this world you will have trouble. But take heart! I have overcome the world."

Jesus knows you and sees the angst you face. He also has personally experienced the grind of daily human life, to in turn help you endure adversities. If we ask Him to come into our hearts and provide focus in the thick of the battle, we receive His wisdom and power to defeat adversity.

In the midst of spiritual warfare, one of the most comforting realities is that my God and Savior has already overcome the world, and He lives in me. The joy of that truth is what makes my life complete. In the midst of the exhaustion, in the midst of the anxiety, there is God giving me the strength to carry on in chaos. I put my life in His hands even when I am feeling far away, even when I've sinned, when I can't see through the fog of war.

I don't know where you are, but you may find yourself engaged in combat with the enemy. He's tempting you to do something you really don't want to do. He's planting thoughts you don't want to think. You may be reaching a point of desperation, exhaustion, ready to give up doing the Christian thing.

This is some of that trouble Jesus promised. But take heart. He has overcome the world. You have a Commander you can trust in the fog of war.

What's confusing you right now? Is it coming from circumstances outside you? Is it coming from within you? Both? Talk to your Commander now. How will you make this part of your life's survival routine?

Memorize: *John 16:33*

The Memorial

Amazing Grace" dripped through the air in the dusty old British gymnasium where we held our memorial service for my first soldier to die, SSG Gary Vaillant. It was as though someone had taken one of those small garden tools with the three prongs and was raking it across my heart. I had to keep telling myself, *Stay strong. Stay strong. Can't let the soldiers see you cry.* A tear leaked from my eye.

The ceremony continued. A psalm was read. I gave the tribute. One of the soldier's friends spoke, and finally my commander spoke. Then we took roll call.

"Staff Sergeant Gary Alexander Vaillant!"

The reply: "He is no longer with us!"

Then the twenty-one-gun salute. I hear gunfire every day, but there was something poetic about firing three volleys with seven rifles.

Sergeant Valliant had died on the first day we officially took over the patrol of the highway and its surrounding towns. I could not believe it. I was watching my men move out into sector, the sun dancing off the tops of the turret, creating heat waves. The 120-degree heat pounded down as I stepped out of my air-conditioned TOC (tactical operations center) and looked over the town of Khalidiyah with its minarets staring back at me. The time we took over the highway was 1400. At 1404, a huge explosion erupted and reached toward the heavens. The explosion caused me to jump. I ran back inside. I tried to discern over the radio what happened. Through the confusion on the radio came three letters that were very clear, and when spoken they caused silence to ripple through the TOC for a moment. K-I-A, killed in action. I quickly threw on my gear and sprinted down to my tank. My gunner was doing some maintenance on the tank, and as soon as he saw me running at a full sprint, he knew something was wrong. He yelled at the driver to get the tank fired up.

"What's wrong, sir?"

"We have a KIA."

We pushed out into sector as fast as the 72-ton, 1600 horsepower, turbine engine could move us, which was 43 mph. As I moved to the gate of the base to go out into sector, another tank was coming back in. It was SSG Vaillant's tank. SGT Olan, the gunner, was now in the hatch. He looked at me with haunted eyes. He took his hand and moved it back and forth over his neck. SSG Vaillant was gone. I had to press the hurt to the back of my mind for a moment. My men were in contact. I needed to be there. Within minutes of leaving the base, we came under machine-gun fire. The insurgents were north of the Euphrates river and we were on the south. They had detonated the roadside bomb, and now were trying inflict more casualties with machine-gun fire. I had three tanks online and we fired round after round at the insurgents. Within moments, we had fire-superiority and the insurgents fled. I sent two tanks across the bridge to the north side of the river. I followed with 100 infantrymen in tow. I dismounted my tank and we began to search and to search and to search. Nine hours of sweating, searching, and of finding nothing of significance. Questions arose. *God, am I going to live through a year of this?* I thought of SSG Vaillant and a tear eclipsed my eyelash.

The real flood of tears came after the memorial. Anytime someone close to you dies, it is very important that you keep their memory alive. You do this by telling stories, recalling events, just reminiscing about better times. I had the men gather in a horseshoe formation around me.

I asked, "Does anyone want to say anything about SSG Vaillant?"

For a moment, there was no response. Everyone just stared at the dirt. Just as the silence started to become awkward, PVT Cavazos spoke.

"Sir, I have something to say," he muttered. He spoke of how SSG Gary Vaillant and he were stranded at a firing range in South Korea before we deployed to Kuwait. They were awaiting transportation, and because it was monsoon season in Korea, it started to rain. They decided to sit back-to-back, Forrest-Gump-and-Bubba style. Gary started talking about Jesus. It was getting late, and PVT Cavazos said to him, "Sergeant, I'm getting tired." SSG Vaillant continued to talk about his amazing love for Jesus. Even though PVT Cavazos tried to stay respectfully awake, he fell asleep with the drizzle on his face. When Cavazos awoke about an hour later, SSG Vaillant had not skipped a beat. He was still talking about the greatest love of his life, Jesus Christ.

I want to be remembered like that.

I want to be remembered as one whose whole life was about one thing—the good news of Jesus Christ. Paul, writing to the Philippian believers, touched often on this life theme. He knew that any day might be his last. He was at all times subjected to dangerous situations for Christ. He never feared for his own life. Instead, his greater concern was that he would have the courage to stand firm for the gospel.

He wrote, "I eagerly expect and hope that I will in no way be ashamed, but will have sufficient courage so that now as always Christ will be exalted in my body, whether by life or by death. For to me, to live is Christ and to die is gain" (Philippians 1:20–21). Paul was remembered for a life dedicated to Christ. That was all he knew.

SSG Gary Vaillant lived a life of danger. The day before his death, SSG Vaillant used his .50-caliber machine gun to destroy two antitank mines—the same type of explosive that killed him and made his tank "non-mission capable" the following day. It was his undaunted courage in the face of fear that forced others to admire SSG Vaillant and his genuine faith. He never cared about public opinion. He cared about the gospel of Jesus Christ. If you were to ask anyone what SSG Vaillant was about, anyone who knew him even briefly would respond, "Jesus Christ."

I want people to talk about me like that. I want people to know that my heart's one desire is Jesus Christ, because my actions reflect that. I want my life to reveal one unyielding devotion.

Every day it boils down to this question: "How can I give Him my heart today?" Jesus calls us to die to self in order that we may be able to give our lives away for Him.

What will people say about you when you die?

What if you were to die tomorrow?

How would you be remembered?

What legacy would you leave?

What indelible mark for Christ would you

impress upon someone?

Who are you living for—

Jesus Christ or yourself?

Giddy as a Schoolgirl

Constant battle can definitely wear on the soul. We long for a time when we don't have to talk about IEDs, snipers, and RPGs.

In the wake of SSG Vaillant's death, I was longing for one of those moments. I had that faraway feeling that comes when you've been beaten down emotionally. I prayed, *Lord, give me someone to talk about You with. I am dying here.*

I walked into my TOC (tactical operation center) and found another captain there who was using it. I am situated in an old Royal Air Force base tower. It was the control tower during the times that the British Air Force was here in the early 1930s, and it provides the best line of sight in the camp. So it also has the best communications range. The other captain saw my *Message* Bible on the table and started reading it. After a moment he asked, "Is this yours?"

I nodded. Then he became giddy as a schoolgirl and talked about how he had never seen anything like it. He went on to explain that his wife had just given birth to his first son, and it forced him to think about some sobering realities. We then talked for about an hour about what it meant to figure out God's will. What an incredible conversation.

As he was talking, I could just feel God. I actually had to hold back the tears. Why was I crying over a conversation about God's will? I was emotionally and spiritually starving, and He fed me. I had been used to feasting in a Christian environment, but now I was in a place where not everyone automatically voiced their love for Jesus. I found my soul very hungry. So in one conversation, God reminded me that He is capable of providing for my needs. I love that.

When I am running on empty, God always comes through. David wrote: "GOD, investigate my life; get all the facts first-hand. I'm an open book to you; even from a distance, you know what I'm thinking. You know when I leave and when I get back; I'm never out of your sight. You know everything I'm going to say before I start the first sentence. I look behind me and you're there, then up ahead and you're there, too—your reassuring presence, coming and going. This is too much, too wonderful—I can't take it all in!" (Psalm 139:1–6, *The Message*).

What a powerful thing it is to know that God knows when I am hurting. He knows when I am at my limit, and I just need a little grace.

Grace. So perfect. So pure. So God. That is what He delivers. Often in life we are running on fumes. No matter how much we desire godliness, we can find ourselves in a rut...or even a desert. Even though all we want is His closeness, we wonder if He hears our cries.

The truth is, He does hear you! He knows what you need. He's more than willing to help. Just ask Him.

Where are you? Are you feeling low, beat down by an unending series of crises? Do you find yourself reeling emotionally and spiritually? Do you feel as though God is not there, or not paying attention? Do you know that Jesus has experienced those same feelings? Did you know all He wants from you is for you to ask Him for help—with an honest heart that acknowledges its weaknesses and need of a Savior?

Remember: *God loves the honest heart.*

Riding the Fence

SEPTEMBER 17, 2004

Fighting the Mujahadin (the anti-Coalition forces) is tough. You cannot tell who is who. The Mujahadin don't wear uniforms. In fact, they will force civilians to work for them against their will. The Mujahadin are able to learn who is working for the Iraqi National Guard or the Iraqi police forces. Then they find their families and sequester them for a while. Usually they coerce their victims into compliance by threats against their family members' lives, or by threatening to sever a limb or gouge out their eyes. The Iraqi National Guardsmen find themselves in a no-win situation. Do they do the right thing and protect the Iraqi people and Coalition forces? Or do they turn their heads while a bomb is placed on the road, endangering those they are sworn to protect and defend?

I find that a lot of these Iraqis ride the fence. They're respectful toward me, to my face, and then respectful to the insurgents to their face. Whoever intimidates most effectively gets the allegiance of these people. As far as I am concerned, someone who works for the Mujahadin is an enemy, and we must arrest or kill anyone we catch in a hostile act. That's the life-and-death reality out here. People will fight against us, sometimes under the coercion of the bad guys, sometimes because they have to feed their family, and sometimes for what they perceive to be honor.

Although it is frustrating, I can actually sympathize. As a Christian, I know the right thing to do a lot of the time. I know right from wrong. I know who my Master is. I am a Christian and my Lord is Jesus. Yet you can catch me at times serving other masters, such as myself and my pride, my lust, my greed, or my laziness. Whenever I knowingly sin, I am drawing a line in the sand and choosing to stand on the side opposing Christ. We are easily intimidated by our spiritual enemy, and we give in to coercion, siding against our Lord.

Jesus knew about this dilemma. He was no fool. He knew how deceitful the heart can be. In Matthew 6:19–34, Jesus spoke right to this matter. He said in verse 21, "For where your treasure is, there your heart will be also." As Americans, we tend to treasure material things. We tend to treasure cars, stereos, boats, and cash. Some of us treasure our relationships. That happens to be one of my weak points—my heart's desire is to be married. When I invest my heart devotion into that desire, then it becomes my treasure; I want to kick myself when that happens. I've chosen to focus on what I don't have, rather than on what I do have—the greatest treasure of all, Jesus Christ, who satisfies completely.

Verse 24 says, "No one can serve two masters. Either he will hate the one and love the other, or he will be devoted to the one and despise the other. You cannot serve both God and Money." Jesus was saying that if you treasure material wealth, you will lose out. It's one master or the other—not both.

Money is only one of many possible masters Jesus could have mentioned here. In the same way, I cannot be a servant of both relationships and God. I have to choose one or the other. That doesn't mean I can never talk to a woman, or that we must all give away all our money. His point was that I become a servant to a relationship, or to money, when I let it use me, rather than my using it as a tool for God. I live as a servant of God when I will use my marital status—whatever it might be…singleness now or "married-ness" in the future—to serve and worship Him.

Verse 33 is the final nail in the coffin on this issue. It summarizes all that I have just written in one sentence: "But seek first his kingdom and his righteousness, and all these things will be given to you as well." God is saying, *If you just seek me first, if you die to yourself, if you are able to struggle and go without something you desire, then I will give you more than you ever dreamed.* God says to me through this verse, *Chris, don't worry about the fact that you are in a combat zone and not around any girls. Don't worry that you have not yet started a family. Trust me and I will give you Myself. Oh, and I'll also give you all these other little things that you desire as well.*

That sounds good. But accepting it requires faith. And you may say you have faith, but you show what you really believe by your actions. The action of seeking God first is living proof of your faith. That is what touches the heart of God.

Do you find yourself riding the fence?
Are you trying to appease both God and the
sinful nature? What is it that you are treasuring?
Is it money? Is it pride? Is it fame? Is it self?
Can you give up all things to seek God?
Can you trust Him for everything else?

Memorize: *Matthew 6:33.*

Left Out

One of the hardest things to do here is physical exercise. Each day I spend out in sector battling the heat, battling the insurgents. An RPG streaks across an alleyway and comes close to one of my tanks. Immediately, I jump up, put on my gear, and head out. I meet my infantrymen on the ground with my interpreter, Muhammad, in tow. We question the people and, when we have evidence, we make the arrests. This process can take several hours of work through the sweltering heat. It seems as if the days sort of run into each other. I have my men develop a log so that we can recall every RPG, IED (roadside bomb), or sniper fire that occurred. Just when one situation is put under control, another one springs up and my mind and body have to put full effort into the confrontation of the enemy. These constant patrols and gun battles can make you so tired that the last thing you want to do is work out. After you let yourself go for a long time, you start to wonder, *What's the point?* You know you'll only work out once, and then skip exercising for several more days. So the lone workout does no good.

In fact, that is the attitude I have had for the past month. But today I broke through with a baby step. I did not go for a full-blown workout as I have in the past. I just made sure I made it into the gym and did a few exercises.

While I did this, I meditated on how this parallels my spiritual conditioning regimen. My pattern is to sin against God, then feel like I'm on His blacklist for a while. I figure I have to stay away from Him until I get my life straightened out. My reasoning goes, *Well, as long as I'm blacklisted, I might as well sin some more.* I avoid going to God. After all, what good is one lone prayer session going to do?

Have you ever thought this way? You are not alone. I know many Christians struggle with this.

Here is the truth of the matter: Jesus came to destroy the religious mentality that doing things right earns God's acceptance, and that if you are not doing right, you are out of the buddy club.

When Jesus came on the scene declaring the Good News that the kingdom was near, people had a certain moralistic expectation of Him. So when He hung out with tax collectors and didn't condemn them, they were flabbergasted. We see the miraculous paradox in God's unconditional acceptance policy when we realize that Matthew and Zacchaeus—both tax collectors, among the worst of sinners—were changed by it. (See Matthew 9:9–11; Luke 19:1–10). Not because Jesus pointed out how screwed up and evil they were. This was already amply clear. They had already been blacklisted by the religious leaders and by the people from whom they stole. They were obviously sinful and there was no disguising it. No, Matt and Zack were changed by grace.

When Jesus comes along, He brings a new concept to light. He doesn't say to those mired in sin, "Stop sinning, get your life on track, start being nice, and then you'll be ready to come to Me. *Then* I will put you on the right spiritual plane." With Matthew and Zacchaeus, we don't even see Him asking them to change. What did He do? In both cases He went to a dinner party at their houses. Jesus revolutionized their lives by means of a love that no one had ever seen before.

At times, we are in the tax collector's shoes. We beat ourselves up so badly that we feel it is going to take a while to get ourselves right with God again. So we give up and hang out in Sinville a little longer. We blacklist ourselves and refuse to let God take us off the list until we "get past this situation" or until we're "ready to do the God-thing over again." We act as if we can earn God's love, as if we need to accomplish certain steps of behavior or penance to get ourselves off the blacklist.

Jesus came to break us of the do-it-yourself, earn-your-own-way mentality. Once Jesus was asked, "What must we do to do the works God requires?" He answered, "The work of God is this: to believe in the one whom he has sent" (John 6:28–29). That is what you have to do. That is the work of God.

This is good news for me, because I have often heard this statement: "If Jesus is not Lord of all, He is not Lord at all." That briefs well, but it is so unbiblical. There are so many parts of my life that I have not surrendered to Christ. When John, James, and Peter started to follow Christ, they were still about as sinful as they come, vying over who would be Jesus' right-hand man. You and I are both sinful too. The one who says he obeys Jesus in everything is a liar. "There is no one righteous, not even one" (Romans 3:10; see also 1 John 1:8).

You may be in one of three places. You might be in a sinful place, feeling trapped on God's blacklist, unworthy to pray, planning to get back to God once you get your life right.

On the other hand, you might think you have it all together and it's everyone else that's all screwed up. (If you really are sinless, e-mail me. Let's do lunch. I'd love to hear how you did it.)

Or you might have come to the realization that all you need

to do is invite Jesus over for dinner, and let Him change you by
His love, His grace, His forgiveness.

*In which of those three "places" are you? If you're
in one of the first two, how can you get to the
third? How do you want God's love to change
you? (Tell Him.)*

Remember: *Nothing can separate us from the
love of God. Read Romans 8:31–38.*

Band of Brothers for Thanksgiving

NOVEMBER 25, 2004

Thanksgiving here at Camp Habbaniyah was a little different than any I have experienced in the past. Not only was it Thanksgiving—it was also the day we decided to celebrate the Marine Corps' birthday. You see, we are a brigade attached to the 1st Marine Division. This is the same division responsible for the Guadalcanal action in World War II. So being under the command structure of the Marines, we were given an opportunity to celebrate with them. And it was the day of initiation into the Currahee Brotherhood.

This is the traditional name of a battalion with a storied history beginning in World War II. If you watched HBO's *Band of Brothers*, then you know the origin of this unit. It was originally the 506th Parachute Infantry Regiment. It participated in the D-Day invasion. It was heralded for honor and bravery at the Battle of the Bulge. In Vietnam, it was among the first air-mobile/air-assault units that conducted large-scale invasions with helicopters. After that, the battalion took its stand on the DMZ between North and South Korea, until we were called upon to come to Iraq to write the next chapter of the Brotherhood's warrior legacy.

All officers of the battalion were initiated into the Brotherhood. The battalion commander presided over the ceremony. The executive officer of the battalion directed the procession, and the company commanders served as judge and jury to determine whether the new officers were worthy to bear the Currahee name.

All of the new officers, including me, were corralled into a back room of the east mess hall. We were given instruction as to how to march and what to chant, and we were given cheat sheets on the Currahee history. During the moment we were given to study, the tension rose as we wondered what the Brotherhood would do to us.

The captains went first. We marched in and stood in front of our judge and jury. We were taunted by the Brotherhood's younger members, while the company commanders eyed us intently. Then the questions began. We were quizzed on the Currahee history, and the exercise soon became more than merely cognitive. Any slight mistake in an answer was punishable by bodily conditioning. We got in a lot of exercise before we finally managed a correct answer and were allowed to step forward. More interrogation, more responses exacted. And finally we were instructed to step up to...the grog.

The grog is a drink concocted from all sorts of disgusting ingredients, and of course the recipe can never be revealed. We were ordered: "Drink!" And, one by one, we drank. As each one finished, we sounded off: "Currahee!"

In that moment, I was transformed from subhuman Currahee-hopeful to Brotherhood warrior of the 506th Infantry Band of Brothers. I went from the one being judged to one who judges. I joined my company commander brethren, and together we called forward the next set of officers to be initiated. I was given a seat of honor, and I was asked to question the next set of newbies trying to enter the Brotherhood. When it was my turn to question these Currahee-hopefuls, I stood before them as if I had been a Currahee my whole life. I asked questions, and when they could not answer correctly, their reward was intense physical exercise. Good times!

After the initiation, I reflected on the event. And I was thankful. It reminded me of my sinful state before I became dedicated to God. It reminded me of the condition of my soul before Christ came and made *me* a son of God! And not only a son, but an *heir*.

Paul wrote the Galatians, "Because you are sons, God sent the Spirit of his Son into our hearts, the Spirit who calls out, 'Abba, Father.' So you are no longer a slave, but a son; and since you are a son, God has made you also an heir. Formerly, when you did not know God, you were slaves to those who by nature are not gods" (Galatians 4:6–8).

What an honor! Just as I gained new status in the Brotherhood, we who have placed our faith in Christ gain new status as members of God's family.

Now, I had to go through an initiation rite in order to qualify to become a Currahee. Otherwise I wasn't good enough. Praise God that becoming a son is a gift and cannot be earned, only received. This is a concept that is hard for many to grasp. A lot of people are attracted to a religion where you have to do something, where keeping rules allows them to feel as though they accomplished enough to earn their own salvation. But God says salvation, and our identity as His children, is a gift.

Even some Christians who have been saved by grace go back to keeping a list of rules, in hopes that God might love them more. Please realize that God cannot love you more. You already have all of His infinite love, and nothing you can do will make Him love you more.

≡

Have you made that part of your worldview?
Are you working as hard as you can to be a good
person in hopes of earning your way to heaven?
Did you once accept Christ by grace, but now
are trying to do more so that God might love
you more? What is it that prevents you from
accepting grace that is free?

My Blasted Pride

SEPTEMBER 23, 2004

The war pushes on. It's strange how war can almost become routine. You get used to the incoming mortars, RPG attacks, and bombs exploding. The pace of battle starts to become commonplace. With routine comes a comfort level where survival sometimes ceases to be your highest priority.

Yesterday, while on patrol, I was notified of a suspicious-looking man. I brought my interpreter to the scene. The man had been eyeing my tanks as though he had hatred coursing through his veins. He was working with a construction team, mixing cement with a shovel. His wiry frame and weathered hands perspired deeply under the duress of the work. I had my squad of infantrymen surround us in order that I might be able to question this man that seemed suspicious. I had Muhammed ask him his name. He didn't answer. I asked the other men working with him what his name was, and they didn't know. I again asked the man his name. He was silent. Clearly, this man was an insurgent. No one hides their identity to coalition forces for nothing. And his entire construction team had no idea who he was. I ordered him detained. We took him back to camp to be further interrogated. It turned out that he had important information regarding anti-Coalition forces, paving the way for the seizure of enemy arms caches.

Good so far. Now here's where my priorities proved to be out of order. Later that day my boss called me on the radio and informed me that a *different* unit had detained this individual.

He praised them up and down.

But that was my guy!

Hey, that was me! I wanted to shout. *I got him. I deserve the credit.* However, I knew that any such remark would probably get me verbally hazed, so I kept my mouth shut. I was burning on the inside as I signed off.

That's when the Holy Spirit gave me a couple smacks in the face. *Why are you so angry that someone else got the credit? You should simply rejoice that good was done.*

Oops! I had to take a quiet moment with God to ask Him to forgive my pride and selfishness. I am a product of America, where we are all very fond of tooting our own horns. After all, if I don't toot it, who's going to toot it for me? The truth is that I have received a lot of credit out here for doing well. For some reason, though, I didn't want anyone to upstage me, to steal a single photon of my spotlight.

In that moment, 1 Samuel 18:6–9 came to mind: "When the men were returning home after David had killed the Philistine, the women came out from all the towns of Israel to meet King Saul with singing and dancing, with joyful songs and with tambourines and lutes. As they danced, they sang: 'Saul has slain his thousands, and David his tens of thousands.' Saul was very angry; this refrain galled him. 'They have credited David with tens of thousands,' he thought, 'but me with only thousands. What more can he get but the kingdom?' And from that time on Saul kept a jealous eye on David."

I felt the Holy Spirit comparing me with Saul. What a bummer. Then my heart turned to one of my favorite books of the Bible, the letter written by James, the half brother of Jesus: "What causes fights and quarrels among you? Don't they come from your desires that battle within you? You want something but don't get it. You kill and covet, but you cannot have what you want. You quarrel and fight.... But he gives us more grace. That is why Scripture says, 'God opposes the proud but gives grace to the humble'" (James 4:1–2, 6).

Why can't I be humble? Why did I, like Saul, become jealous? I don't know if any of you find yourselves in this predicament at work, at school, or at home. Our own reputation and renown can take over, and we don't even realize it. Often we are the last to recognize how selfish, prideful, and conceited we are. For the Christian, this can severely hamper our ability to share the gospel.

*Do you ever find yourself becoming jealous
when someone else gets your credit
or when someone else is doing well?
Do you ever find your heart becoming hard, like
Saul's, towards another brother or
sister in Christ because you fear they
may receive more notoriety than you?
How has jealousy affected your ability
to shine as a light in the darkness?*

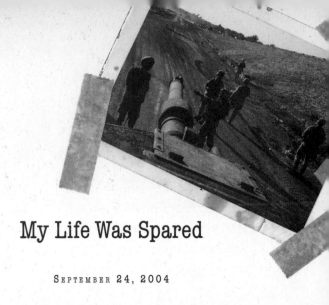

My Life Was Spared

Highway 10 connects several towns between the major cities of Fallujah and Ramadi, one of which is a little town called Khalidiyahh. Yesterday I was on patrol, and I noticed a suspicious taxicab parked on the side of the road. I U-turned my tank and drove toward it. As soon as they saw my tank approach, the men in the taxi hurried to push the broken-down car off the road. Content that the taxi was no longer a potential threat, I turned my attention back to continuing the mission. I drove across the highway median.

BOOM!

An IED went off not two feet from my tank. I was startled for a moment. Then my training kicked in, and I scanned to find the triggerman. I saw a guy running away from the scene and into a nearby house. I quickly called my infantry platoon to search it. Meanwhile I provided "overwatch" from my tank. I then hopped off my tank to investigate further.

We went into the house where the man had darted. We found the man that had run off and we tackled him. We arrested him, but later found out that he was not the triggerman, but a hapless civilian walking down the road in the vicinity of a roadside bomb. We searched the houses in that area and found nothing of interest. After the search was complete, I returned to the median where the IED (Improvised Explosive Device) had exploded. I climbed down into the crater; it was about chest-deep and three feet in diameter.

Three feet of pavement. This was a huge blast.

Questions occupied my mind as I returned to base. Why did my tank survive the explosion without a scratch? Other explosions, neither farther from nor nearer to the tanks they targeted, had killed one of my soldiers and had given another a serious head wound.

Here I am without a scratch.

There's no doubt that it was God's sovereign protection that spared me (see Psalm 91). But why me? I love Psalm 139:1–6. It came to my mind now: "O Lord, you have searched me and you know me. You know when I sit and when I rise, you perceive my thoughts from afar. You discern my going out and my lying down; you are familiar with all my ways. Before a word is on my tongue you know it completely, O Lord. You hem me in—behind and before; you have laid your hand upon me. Such knowledge is too wonderful for me, too lofty for me to attain."

Such knowledge is too wonderful for me, but in my heart I ask God, *Who am I that you would even know my name?* My mind turns to 2 Samuel 9:8 where Mephibosheth, the crippled son of Jonathan and grandson of King Saul, was brought to David's court. Mephibosheth was of royal descent, which, in any other kingdom, would mean he would be killed to ensure that he would not rise up and try to usurp the new king's authority. In this case, King David did a strange thing. Because of his love for Jonathan, David treated Mephibosheth as a son. This move completely astonished everyone. Mephibosheth was joyfully dumbfounded, not able to fully comprehend why his life had been spared. I knew how he felt.

How am I to ever understand? I don't get it. I have no control over many of my life's most important events. I don't understand why good or why bad happens. As far as I can tell, it's just as the bumper sticker notes: "Stuff happens" (my printable paraphrase).

That's when the Holy Spirit opened my heart and led me on to Proverbs 3:5–6. And this powerful passage seemed to make everything fall into its natural order. "Trust in the LORD with all your heart and lean not on your own understanding; in all your ways acknowledge him, and he will make your paths straight." The essence of the Christian faith is this: trusting our heavenly Father with everything. Trusting Him to be in control, and, conversely, understanding that we are not in control. We do not need to know the answers to everything because He is a perfect Father, and we can trust Him with our lives.

My question as to why I was spared yesterday may never be answered on this earth. But I know my Father has an amazing plan for me. Only one important question remains that I can answer: Will I give Him my trust?

How about you? Are you at a place where you need to trust God? When God calls, are you able to give Him your whole heart?

Every Careless Word

You know how it can happen. Just a little sarcasm. Nothing serious. Never intending to hurt anyone's feelings. But you do.

Just today I found out that was me.

Sergeant Oates is one of the strongest Christian men in my company. He hadn't come to church in a while, so one day I said to him, "Hey, missed you at church today."

He replied, "Yeah, I know. I got my time in with God, though."

"I see how it is. You're becoming just another one of those guys who does church on his own. That's cool. I guess the whole body of Christ being the church really isn't that important to you."

Now, when I said that, I was totally kidding. I even had a smile on my face. But for the next week he avoided me like the plague. I got word through some non-Christians that he was upset with me because I offended him. That hurt.

Here we are Christian brothers in a war zone, and I am clueless to the fact that I hurt his feelings. Not only that, but the dirty laundry of Christ's followers was aired for all to see. With one careless comment, I became deserving of the labels that non-believers often give us. Self-righteous. Hypocrite.

But I was just teasing. Do you ever do that? Just joking around. Just a little hee-hee. A little ha-ha. And then you watch your little joke grow up, move back home, and beat you up.

Without you even knowing it, "a little fun" puts a major rift in a friendship. God never intended for our tongues to be used that way. Thank God, Sergeant Oates is twelve years older than me and very mature. So he was willing to approach me about it. We talked it through. I apologized and we are now reconciled.

But there would have been no need for damage control if I had just followed the heart of God.

Paul, in Ephesians 4:29–30, makes this clear. "Do not let any unwholesome talk come out of your mouths, but only what is helpful for building others up according to their needs, that it may benefit those who listen. And do not grieve the Holy Spirit of God, with whom you were sealed for the day of redemption." How did I build up Sergeant Oates? I didn't. How many other soldiers heard me and thought I was serious? Not only did I fail to benefit Sergeant Oates—my joking may have hurt other soldiers whose preconceptions of Christians as hypocrites were justified. And the Holy Spirit was grieved.

I blew it big time. Just a simple comment. Just trying to be funny.

It only takes a spark to burn down a forest. (See James 3:5–6.)

How about you? Have you ever been in this
situation? Do you make a habit of "joking," only
to find that you've crushed someone's feelings?
Do you ever do that to your husband or wife, or
to someone else you love? Have you done it with

Christians? With non-Christians? Where will you draw the line?

Remember: *"The good man brings good things out of the good stored up in him, and the evil man brings evil things out of the evil stored up in him. But I tell you that men will have to give account on the day of judgment for every careless word they have spoken. For by your words you will be acquitted, and by your words you will be condemned"* (Matthew 12:35–37).

Earth Suit

September 28, 2004

Next time you're in your bedroom, I want you to take a look around. If you are like me, you have some clothes thrown on the bed, or lying on the floor. If you are Mr. or Mrs. or Miss (or Ms.) Clean-and-Tidy, they're all hung up or folded in drawers.

Now take a look at your skin. You may be brown, white, black, or whatever. Feel your bones. Feel their hardness. Touch your temples and feel the guardian of what is captured within—your soul. Just as your clothes cover your body, your body covers your soul. Your body is nothing more than an earth suit.

On the night of September 28, this reality became embedded in my mind and stirred within me an intense physical and emotional reaction. It was about 11 p.m., and the whole day had been quiet. The crack of the radio made my ears prick up.

"Apache Tango, Apache 2-2, IED at the 5-3-9."

The response: "Apache 2-2, casualties? Are there any casualties?"

No answer.

"Apache 2-2, this is Apache Five [my executive officer]. Do you have any casualties?"

After a pause that seemed an eternity, I heard, "Yes."

My executive officer pried for more information. "Where are the casualties?"

The platoon sergeant, SFC Stemen, interjected, "Apache

2-2, this is Apache 2-4. Get on the %&*^-ing net and give us a SITREP!" (That's a "situation report.")

Finally the response: "The loader is KIA."

As soon as I heard that, I bolted for my tank, frantic that my crew was not there to meet me. I paced about, wondering what could have happened. When my gunner arrived, I looked at him angrily. "Where were you? We have a KIA!"

He looked at me a little surprised. It had only been about seven minutes from the time they had been alerted till the time they got to the tank. My gunner didn't say a word, but got in the tank. I knew I had offended him, but I didn't care. We had another soldier killed in action. As we pulled the tank out of the airplane hangar that housed it, my gunner whispered over the tank intercom, "Sir, you have got to keep it together. We need you to keep it together."

Clarity returned to my mind and I prepared myself for what I was about to see. I kept patting my gunner on the shoulder and saying, "It's going to be okay. It's going to be okay."

I think I said that more for myself than I did for anyone else on the tank. We drove the seventy-two-ton tank at forty-three miles per hour—as fast as the 1600-horsepower, turbine engine could carry us—through the streets of Khalidiyahh, past the town of Modique and to the scene of my soldier's death. When I arrived on the scene, I jumped off the tank and told my gunner to grab the shotgun and come with me. He was seasoned and had seen dead men before. I also told him to grab a shovel. This could be really bad.

One of my infantry lieutenants, Lt Brandon Anderson, met me on the ground and guided me to my young private. I tried to go through the mental preparations of encountering death to face what I knew was about to confront me.

The first thing that hit me was the smell. It was the pungent, unmistakable smell of death. A combination of blood and dead flesh. My stomach turned, and I willed myself to walk forward in spite of the nausea.

Then I saw him. I had my night-vision goggles on. The night-vision goggles use the ambient light of stars or of any other natural light to give you vision. However, everything is green. I looked through the green to see something I thought I might see on *Silence of the Lambs*. The blast had catapulted him probably thirty feet in the air and threw him about twenty feet across the pavement. He lay in a formless heap. I could not recognize him as that funny kid who was always laughing and joking. I could not recognize him as human. I picked through the pieces. I found his spinal column and his ribs totally detached from his body. There was no head. For a moment, I wanted to just walk away and forget that this ever happened. As these thoughts were ravaging my mind, my medic pulled up in his tracked ambulance. It looked like a mini-tank, only it didn't have a gun on it and its only purpose was to haul off casualties. A million things ran through my mind as I looked at the skin that used to contain one of my beloved soldiers. As I continued to survey his crumpled body, my million things turned into one dominant thought: *Ashes to ashes, dust to dust.* All that remained was his earth suit.

Sergeant Kassa, my medic, a man earning his citizenship from Africa by being in the U.S. Army, picked up all the pieces feverishly as if time was of the essence. Time was of the essence. Insurgents were watching us as we tried to gather our hearts and keep our minds and wits about us. I moved over to a metal sign that read, "Americans leave this country or you will all die." I picked it up and carried it over to the medic track.

Sergeant Kassa started putting the pieces into a black body bag. As he zipped up the body bag, I thought of eternity. I thought of my own death. I thought of my men and what could be their deaths. Everything suddenly became very clear.

This is not our home. We were made in God's image. God is Spirit, and these earthen bodies we wear provide a dwelling place for His image and His likeness. Yet as Americans we sometimes take that for granted. I think we Americans can become comfortable in the security that we enjoy. Living life as God intended takes a backseat to our own agendas and our own desires. Some live to accumulate wealth. Some live to have a nice family and to be nice people, not ever wanting to hurt anyone. However, we lose sight of what God has in store for us. Few Christians consciously think, *Who cares about the world? I am looking out for number one.* But we have been subtly taught that life is about me, and I have to get mine. So we make all kinds of plans for living out our agendas, for living up to the Western idea of success.

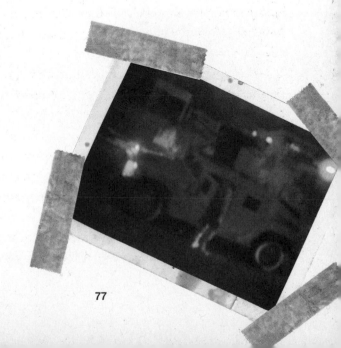

James 4:13–15 says, "Now listen, you who say, 'Today or tomorrow we will go to this or that city, spend a year there, carry on business and make money.' Why, you do not even know what will happen tomorrow. What is your life? You are a mist that appears for a little while and then vanishes. Instead, you ought to say, 'If it is the Lord's will, we will live and do this or that.'"

Listen to James. "If it is the Lord's will, we will live…" James speaks directly to those who are all about our own plans for the future. How can you count on your humanly conceived plan when you don't know what the Lord's will is? You may not live until tomorrow. In the time that you are guaranteed—that is, this moment—you must live to the full for Jesus Christ. It is that simple. God has an agenda. Our lives may be cut short at any moment to fulfill His agenda.

Our prayers tend to be one-way conversations. They are like Christmas wish lists, as if God were Santa Claus and His answer was based on whether we were naughty or nice. God is not like that! He is a perfect Father who loves us. His desire is to commune with us, to get into our hearts, to tell us what we need to know about His agenda.

We miss that. We miss the "His agenda" aspect. The Bible says in Matthew 6:8 that God already knows what you need before you ask. So why even pray? We pray because, more than anything, God wants us to live out His agenda. He wants us to align our wills with His and to conduct ourselves in a manner that is worthy of Him. That doesn't necessarily mean that we sell everything we have, give it to the homeless shelter, and take up residence there ourselves. But it does mean that we stop thinking we are at the center of the universe. We die to self so that we can truly live. We learn to do this day by day. It won't happen overnight. And the godly life will be hard at times, but that doesn't mean we have to quit. This life is so short. It's just a little ways to the finish line.

Josh—my soldier who died—was only twenty. You have a 100-percent chance of following him one day, when your body returns to dust. My prayer is that you will look to God's agenda and not your own as you live in this earth suit.

Who is at the core of your life? Is it you?
Do you view life like one big movie with you as
the star, and your friends and family playing
supporting roles? When you pray, do you ever
ask God what His agenda is? His agenda for the
people you work with, live with, and love?
Can you take a step downstage and let God
become the star?

Jesus vs Jenna Jameson

OCTOBER 7, 2004

If you walk through any combat barracks, you are going to find one thing dominating the walls—hot, scantily clad chicks. Researchers are still trying to understand this phenomenon. Soldiers in the middle of nowhere will post women on their walls.

Throughout the past few weeks of death and heartache, I have noticed something else appearing alongside the ladies— Bible verses. Not just in one or two rooms, but consistently displayed everywhere in the company. Right next to Carmen Electra is Jeremiah 29:11–13. Beside Jenna Jameson is 1 Corinthians 10:13. Beyonce is next door to John 3:16. (I am not sure if churches have caught on that this could be a new way of motivating Scripture memorization, but I think it is bound to catch on.)

Jesus' voice is speaking more loudly inside the hearts of

these men, raising questions. Christ is becoming real. The powerful Word of God is calling out, inviting these soldiers to no longer be slaves of sin, but to become sons of God. An anthem is rising, appealing for a change of allegiance.

The battle of flesh versus spirit has begun. There is something undeniable when God calls you. You can ignore His call for only so long, until it beats on your heart like a war chief on his tom-tom. The physical conflict is on the battlefield; the spiritual battle is in the heart.

The parable of the sower comes to mind. Jesus taught, "A farmer went out to sow his seed. As he was scattering the seed, some fell along the path, and the birds came and ate it up. Some fell on rocky places, where it did not have much soil. It sprang up quickly, because the soil was shallow. But when the sun came up, the plants were scorched, and they withered because they had no root. Other seed fell among thorns, which grew up and choked the plants. Still other seed fell on good soil, where it produced a crop—a hundred, sixty or thirty times what was sown" (Matthew 13:3–8).

I want to focus on the second and third types of seed—that which fell on rocky soil and that which fell amongst the weeds. Jesus explained later, in verses 20–22, "The one who received the seed that fell on rocky places is the man who hears the word and at once receives it with joy. But since he has no root, he lasts only a short time. When trouble or persecution comes because of the word, he quickly falls away. The one who received the seed that fell among the thorns is the man who hears the word, but the worries of this life and the deceitfulness of wealth choke it, making it unfruitful."

I get excited when I see Bible verses spring up among my men. However, I wonder inwardly if this is just for comfort's sake, but doesn't indicate that a heart transplant has taken place. I see these guys thinking this Jesus thing is great, but they quickly lose interest. There is no depth. No real piercing of the heart. Jesus is just another cool thing to put on the wall next to Janet Jackson.

Then I look at my own life and observe how many times I have mental pictures of women stapled in the walls of my mind, right next to my favorite Bible verses. Sometimes I also let worries about marriage, worries of survival on the battle-field, or worries of command responsibilities interfere my true pursuit—my pursuit of the heart of Jesus Christ.

A shallow, cluttered life. I can say that all I want is Jesus, that He is my everything. But if you were to sift through the soil of my brain, sometimes you wouldn't have to dig very deep to reach bottom. And you would find some well-rooted weeds growing there, choking out my fruitfulness, rendering me inca-pable of bringing God's kingdom to this earth.

Some of us have hearts filled with rocky soil, and we think this Jesus experience is cool. But maybe we're not so ready to give our hearts completely to Christ. Others of us are sold out to Christ, but are not multiplying the kingdom because we are smothered by sin and worry.

Where are you? Have you deeply committed yourself to Christ? Do you let the worries of life choke you out? Have you let Christ pierce your heart? Have you given Him control?

Engine Shutdown

October 15, 2004

So there I was, out in sector. I had just completed my mission—namely, to make my way to an informant's house undetected and find out why he wanted to talk to me. So I drove near his house and dismounted my tank. I took the battalion scout platoon leader, Ryan Davis; my infantry platoon leader, Ben Simmonette; and Muhammed, my interpreter, with me. We first entered a nearby house, asked some pointed questions about anti-Coalition involvement, and performed a light search of the house. I then went to the roof with the scout to "overwatch" the informant's house and wait for the cover of darkness. As soon as darkness descended, we bid the family of this house adieu and crept through a hole in a wall that took us to the informant's house. All the lights were out, and no one appeared to be home. However, I had an inkling he would be there, and our patience paid off. The door soon opened.

The man invited us in and gave us all the information he had. He provided some amazing leads and showed us on a map where the bad guys were. When we were finished, we covertly left and made our way through the darkness to my tank. We discussed our exfiltration plan and waited for the Humvees to take the scout and infantry lieutenants away. I hopped on my tank and headed back to the forward operating base.

Things seemed to be going fine when all of a sudden we started slowing down.

"Hey, Mendez, is your grandmother driving here? Let's go," I quipped.

"I'm trying," Mendez replied, and then all systems turned off. No power in the turret. No power in the tank. We could not move. We were paralyzed.

Thankfully, the radios worked, and I called back to base requesting the tank tow truck (an M88) to rescue my tank.

There is something eerie about being out in sector with no power to your tank, especially when you are stopped in an area that is notorious for IEDs. Muhammed, who was in the tank with me, shouted in good but broken English, "This @#$% tank! It @#$!"

Then over the radio came a Jamaican voice that I have come to love. SSG Williams said, "Hey, sir, I can come down there and provide you local security if you would like."

Would I ever, I thought. "Roger."

SSG Williams and his crew stayed with me for about forty-five minutes while Muhammad continued to give me his thoughts on the value of my tank. Finally the M88 arrived and we were extremely excited to get moving. SSG Williams' pres-

ence was a great comfort. He willingly put himself in danger for me for no other reason than to provide me reassurance, comfort, and security.

In life we need people like that. We need people willing to take risks and give of themselves for those who need a hand.

Job needed such friends as much as anyone. He lost everything. Nothing as temporary or relatively inconsequential as turret and hull power. He lost social status, he lost all of his children, he lost his wife's respect, he lost most of his friends, he lost all of his vast wealth. Pretty much everything.

When his few remaining friends did finally show up, they didn't come simply to hang out and empathize; they offered up every possible reason why he was screwed up. This was not exactly the comfort that Job needed. In Job 6:21, Job described the kind of friends that his "buddies" had turned out to be: "Now you too have proved to be of no help; you see something dreadful and are afraid."

Much of the time, people in crisis don't want your advice—especially when the shock and pain is fresh and raw. They don't want your counsel. They just want you to care. They want someone to understand. They want sincere love.

I was listening to a friend of mine this week talk about how his wife is leaving him. What do I know about marriage? I am not married, but I made all the right sounds and listened and said, "That sucks" a lot. He was not looking for a solution; he was just looking for someone's attention and love.

Romans 12:9–10, 13, 15 says, "Love must be sincere.... Be devoted to one another in brotherly love. Honor one another above yourselves.... Share with God's people who are in need.... Rejoice with those who rejoice; mourn with those who mourn."

*Do you leave your friends to face their pain
powerless and alone? Or do you go to them
and lift them up? Are you willing to encourage
someone who is down, or do you delight in
watching their failures, in order to make
you feel better about yourself? Do you rejoice
with those who rejoice and mourn with
those who mourn? Look deep into your heart
and be honest with yourself and God.*

Search Again

I was in my tank today, patrolling a residential neighborhood that has a high bad-guy concentration. My mission was to take pictures of a suspected bad-guy house. There were rumors that the man who owned the house had fled to Syria to escape our clutches. A thorough search of the house turned up nothing. In fact, since the owner had fled, his house had obviously been robbed of anything of worth.

After completing that mission, I continued my patrol. I noticed a beat-up, white, 1995 pickup with a license number that one of my informants had given me the previous night. The truck had been carrying a sniper to and from his point of fire. I radioed to one of the Humvees patrolling behind me to detain the vehicle. Maneuvering deftly, the Humvee passed me and pulled in front of the white pickup. I ordered that the driver be put in the Humvee with my interpreter, and we went to the driver's house.

Upon arriving at the house, we searched every nook and cranny. We demanded that the man whom we had detained tell us the locations of any weapons, but he held to his contention that he had none. When we found weapons and ammunition everywhere, he gave us a how'd-that-get-there look.

Whenever the men finished searching a room, I had another set of eyes go through it again, and strangely enough, we often found more contraband. This is normal. The first time you go through a room, you don't find everything. The second time, you still don't always find everything. Several attempts may be required in order make a thorough search. From that house we confiscated over one hundred shotgun rounds, about two hundred sniper bullets, several AK-47s, some sniper equipment, and some American cash. Needless to say, we sent that guy up the river.

As I was wading through this contraband, an insight about the Bible crossed my mind. Many times I have missed treasures of wisdom upon the first reading of a Bible passage. Sometimes I've read a passage two or three times in the NIV, and then read it again in *The Message*, and I would surface with a new nugget of truth. At least it was new to me. I had just discovered it. But in reality it had been there the whole time. It was just hidden by my presumption that I already knew that text. That's why I like reading in different translations; it gets me closer to the experience of reading the text for the first time.

Sometimes when conducting a Bible study, one of my soldiers will share how a Bible verse has impacted him. His insight can often relay to me a new truth, because his fresh eyes will pick up on something that my eyes missed.

The benefit of a new translation or a fresh set of eyes is priceless. God calls us to search for wisdom as if given a treasure map to endless bounty. This perspective prevents the perception that the Bible is boring. If the Bible ever becomes boring, it will dry up as a source of wisdom—not because God's Word is any less rich, but because our passion for truth has taken a nap. In Proverbs 2:1–5, Solomon wrote, "My son, if you accept my words and store up my commands within you, turning your ear to wisdom and applying your heart to understanding, and if you call out for insight and cry aloud for understanding, and if you look for it as silver and search for it as hidden treasure, then you will understand the fear of the LORD and find the knowledge of God."

Do you want to know God better? Is your heart searching for the secrets of God? Has the Bible become mundane and so "blah" that it is not worth reading anymore?

The Bible is God's love letter to you. When you receive a passionate letter from a girlfriend, boyfriend, or spouse, you read it over and over again, analyzing why she said this or that, trying to figure out what he really meant there. Basking in the "company" of your loved one. Now think of your beloved as speaking Greek or Hebrew as his or her native tongue. Now you have to learn that language or have your letter translated by a trustworthy interpreter. And multiple translators will bring new light to your loved one's intended meaning. The more varied your perspective on the letter, the better you can discern your lover's heart.

> *Let us not become weary in our search to know*
> *God better. Continue to seek Him in His Word*
> *daily. Turn the various English words and*
> *phrases over in your head and meditate on them.*
> *I promise you will encounter the living God.*

When Life Drops a Bomb

October 30, 2004

Yesterday started out calmly. I was chatting with my dad on the Internet, trying to figure out my webcam and all the trials and tribulations that such technology entails. In the midst of my high-tech troubles, I noticed that the voices on the radios had struck that this-means-trouble pitch.

"IED! Vehicle-borne IED! Casualties unknown."

I ceased work on the Webcam and started putting on my body armor, radio, and weapon. I went down to my tank, ordered the interpreter into the Bradley with a small dismount team, and then I moved out into sector. I pulled up to the site of the vehicle-borne IED. All that remained of the car was the engine block. That was it. Thank God, the driver ran into a tank. The crew within didn't even feel the blow. They heard the loud explosion behind them, and the intense heat gave the tank commander a minor burn.

I gathered evidence around the vehicle. I took pictures and interrogated people in the vicinity. When I finished, along with the rest of the team, I returned to my tank. Another report came over the radio. Our informant was signaling to one of my observation posts that he wanted to talk to me. I made my way toward the informant's home, jumped off the tank, and led a fire team through some weeds, following what I thought might be an insurgent foot path. I climbed over a wall into my informant's back yard. Just as I arrived, I heard a frantic voice on the radio.

"Sniper! We have been hit by sniper! We need to MEDE-VAC!"

I told my interpreter to explain our sudden departure. We would be back here later that night. I weaved my tank through the small residential area—a real trick, because tanks don't generally weave well. I hurried toward an observation post on top of an abandoned house overlooking the sector. This was where the injured soldier had been posted. I found a place to dismount and followed my infantry platoon leader, Lt Ben Jackman, into a nearby house where the sniper had been. We cleared it, trying to find the sniper, but to no avail.

Once I was sure that the enemy had left the area and security was established, I checked on our hurt soldier. He was bleeding profusely from the neck; a medic wearing bloody surgical gloves tended to his wound. We clearly needed to get him out of there. The medic directed us, and I played my part, following his instruction. "We need to get him on the stretcher. Somebody hold his head!" I formed my hands around the wounded man's head and looked straight into his eyes. I prayed aloud, "Dear Jesus, please heal him." And, "In the name of Jesus, be healed." He lurched in pain as we moved him onto the stretcher.

"Sergeant," he gasped, his glassy, bloodshot eyes rolling aimlessly, searching for his leader. "Sergeant, tell my wife I love her."

"Shut up. You are not going to die," came the retort.

"Sergeant, it hurts…" he whispered, breathing labored.

"I know…I know…" came the worried response.

"I love you, Sergeant."

"I love you too."

We moved him to the Bradley, put him inside, and sent him off to the hospital.

I took a deep breath, then went back to my tank. I moved back to the base and started preparing for another informant intelligence gathering mission. Life continues in this business. Things can happen so fast. You know, life can be like yesterday. One moment you are on top of an observation post, and the next you are writhing in pain because you have been shot. One moment you are having a conversation about chow; the next, your tank gets hit by a bomb. One moment you are talking about webcams, and the next moment you are evacuating a casualty of war. Maybe you are not facing literal bombs and bullets. But what about that bomb that was dropped on you when you found out she was pregnant. Or that your spouse or parent has cancer. Maybe you lost your job, or your fiancé just isn't interested anymore. It's Life Interrupted.[2] There is no time to prepare. Things were sailing along as you had planned, and suddenly life is out of control.

That was the story of Job's life. He had it all. Then lost it all. After his first three "friends" finished—quite unhelpfully—ridiculing him, Job's fourth friend, Elihu, gave him some sound advice: "God does all these things to a man—twice, even three times—to turn back his soul from the pit, that the light of life may shine on him" (Job 33:29–30).

Paul also experienced a rude interruption to his plans. He called it "a thorn in my flesh, a messenger of Satan, to torment me" (2 Corinthians 12:7). We're not sure what bomb dropped into Paul's life, but he begged God repeatedly to remove it. Instead of saying yes, God said, "My grace is sufficient for you, for my power is made perfect in weakness" (v. 9). And that's when Paul began to see the value of his unexpected bombs and sniper bullets: "Therefore I will boast all the more gladly about my weaknesses, so that Christ's power may rest on me. That is why, for Christ's sake, I delight in weaknesses, in insults, in hardships, in persecutions, in difficulties. For when I am weak, then I am strong" (v. 10).

Has a bomb been dropped on your life? Are you blaming God or demanding of Him an explanation for this evil? Have you lost hope in His power? His wisdom? His love? Let Christ's power work perfectly through your weakness. Turn it all over to God, so that His light of abundant life might shine on you and through you into the world.

EDITOR'S NOTE: Since the original printing of this book, the young trooper, SPC Collins, has recovered. He was shot through the neck, but there was only minor damage to the arteries.

Getting Through

November 1, 2004

One of the hardest things in this war is arresting the men of a family. (We rarely if ever arrest the women, because in this society women are seen as incapable of carrying out terrorist activities—or any other task outside the home, for that matter.) When I arrest all the men in a family, I am taking away all of the caretakers.

Now, sometimes I'm sure the women think, "Phew! I'm finally rid of that jerk." But most often the women start wailing. And not just any wailing. We're talking about the kind of all-out expression of grief that I've only seen in Middle Eastern cultures. Biblical wailing. The women beat their breasts, tear their clothes, and wipe ash on their faces.

This past week, when I arrested a kid who was about fifteen, his older sister completely lost it. As we started to take him away, this woman clung to her brother like her life depended on him. Maybe it did. It didn't matter to her that their house was filled with terrorist paraphernalia. She only understood that her brother was being taken, and she went berserk. After we pried her fingers away from the boy, she started to beat herself. She hit her face with clenched fists as hard as she could. She then grabbed her face as if it were a mask and started pulling on it until I saw the red of her eye sockets. It was disgustingly horrifying. I tried to stop her from abusing herself, but I couldn't. She could not understand my words. How could I explain that, under American justice, her brother was probably

Mrs. Nina Maachek.

94

just going to be questioned and then released? I couldn't. For all she knew, we were just like Saddam's thugs in the old days, and her brother would never come back.

I asked God what I could do to help this woman, and the answer came in a resounding, silent push on my heart. *Pray.*

Even in America, where we speak the same language, it's sometimes so hard to get past barriers of misunderstanding, misperception, grief, resentment. Even when you don't see someone throwing a physical tantrum, inside they might still be raging and storming, and breaking through the walls of passive aggression, silence, and avoidance and be humanly impossible to reach. That's why you have to fall back on the One who is superhuman. Often, in order to reach a person with the love of Christ, your only answer is prayer.

That's one reason Paul wrote to the young pastor Timothy, "I urge...that requests, prayers, intercession and thanksgiving be made for everyone...that we may live peaceful and quiet lives in all godliness and holiness" (1 Timothy 2:1–2). He knew that we all need God's help to live well with everyone around us, whether it's a civil leader, a neighbor, a sibling, or simply someone whose path you cross at the grocery store.

Does prayer seem too simple an answer? Think about it. For someone who, for whatever reason—deep grief, guilt, or confusion—has turned off their mental faculties, no amount of reasoning can fix it. Certainly it's right to try reasoning and showing love; those go a long way. But for some, they don't go far enough by themselves. We still must not give up; and we have to trust that the situation is not too hard for God.

God knows about your husband who doesn't want to hear about Christ. God knows about the people you work with who constantly give you a hard time about your faith. God knows about the people at church who are self-absorbed and manipulative.

Some may feel outright hate toward you, even though you want to get along with them. You don't want to be enemies, but they seem to leave you no choice. And you've been so badly hurt that you're tempted to start responding in kind. It's with those individuals in mind that Jesus taught, "You have heard that it was said, 'Love your neighbor and hate your enemy.' But I tell you: Love your enemies and pray for those who persecute you, that you may be sons of your Father in Heaven" (Matthew 5:43–45).

You can't create this kind of love by yourself. Step away and pray. Invite God to change your heart, so that you can view them with His eyes, no matter what they do to you. And ask God to change their hearts too. He can. And He just might, if you ask.

Who in your life seems beyond your reach,
beyond reason? With whom do you have a
sandpaper relationship—always rough? Who
do you wish revenge upon, because they've
misunderstood you and have hurt you deeply?
They're the ones to pray for. Why not now?

Move Out of My Way!

According to standard operating procedure, before entering sector, we always conduct a test fire with all of our weapon systems. For this purpose, we use a "test fire pit," where a large dirt berm (or mound) safely absorbs our rounds. Soldiers also use the pit for target practice, so when we pull up, we often have to wait for those using it to move out of the way before conducting test fire.

The other day I was getting ready to roll out into sector with my wingman. I was slightly annoyed to see other soldiers using the test-fire pit, but I waved one of the soldiers over and told him to please have everyone move out. He acknowledged me and then went back to talk to his leadership. I noticed that the patch on his shoulder signified that he was a reserve soldier.

I expected them to stop shooting, move out of the way, and let me fire and leave. Didn't happen. Instead they started another round of firing. For a moment I was calm. Then my head was suddenly filled with raging thoughts: *Are you letting these reservists tell you what to do? You are about to go out on the mean streets where death and mayhem await, and these punks are telling you to wait for them? You are a company commander! Who do these people think they are? Don't let them run over you!*

I am not sure where that voice came from, but I am pretty sure it was not the Holy Spirit. Why I listened, I don't know. I jumped down from the tank as if stung by a swarm of bees. I started yelling at the top of my lungs.

"You!" I pointed. "Move! Now! Let's go!"

Soldiers started scurrying everywhere. I saw the unit's first sergeant and said to him, "Dude! Let's go! I need to get into sector! I have priority! Now get your men out of here!"

He looked at me calmly, but was obviously put off. "Sir, all you had to do was ask. You don't have to talk to us like that."

"Whatever." I walked off. As I returned to my tank, my men were cheering. They thought I was awesome. I really took care of business. I put those reservists in their place. But to be honest, I don't know why I acted like that. I was in no real hurry. I am not normally an impulsive-anger kind of guy.

The next voice I heard was unmistakably the Holy Spirit's. *Do you feel really big now? Do you feel important? Does it make you feel good to make all of these others feel small?*

I am thankful to know that there are men in the Bible who made similar mistakes. Guys with pretty high spiritual pedigrees have lost it when they should have maintained composure. At one point in his commendable leadership career, Moses made a gross error, failing to control his temper. The whiny Israelites were getting to him again. Their lack of faith and continual complaining ripped into his heart so that he acted out of spiritual conceit. However, he received far more than a verbal rebuke from the Holy Spirit; he was sentenced to wander in the desert for the rest of his life.

In the moment, I'm sure Moses felt justified in his rash behavior. Time after time God has miraculously provided for Israel. But here they were again, complaining that they had no water to drink. And blaming Moses for it. So Moses did what he was trained to do—he took the issue to God.

On one previous occasion, God had instructed Moses to strike a particular rock with his staff, and water came out of the rock for the thirsty people. But this time, God said, "Take the staff, and you and your brother Aaron gather the assembly together. Speak to that rock before their eyes and it will pour out its water. You will bring water out of the rock for the community so they and their livestock can drink" (Numbers 20:8).

Now somewhere between talking to God and giving water to the people, Moses had time to think about the situation. I am wondering if Moses started hearing the same voice that filled my head the other morning. *Hey, Moses, these people don't respect you. They don't care that you carry the burden of leadership for them. They think you're a bad leader. They have no real heart for God. They don't deserve to live.* In any case, Moses worked himself into a lather.

"So Moses took the staff from the Lord's presence…gathered the assembly together in front of the rock and Moses said to them, 'Listen, you rebels, *must we* bring you water out of this rock?' Then Moses raised his arm and struck the rock twice with his staff. Water gushed out, and the community and their livestock drank" (vv. 9–11, emphasis mine).

Caught up in his position, Moses gave full vent to his frustration. His error was believing and declaring that it was he and Aaron who brought the water from the rock, rather than giving credit to God. And instead of obeying God's instruction to speak to the rock, he fell back on his own strategy and his own strength. He swung his staff with home-run force and bashed the rock in an expression of absolute disgust for these people. Maybe he was also venting frustration with God.

Here was a miracle from God, and Moses treated it with contempt. God wanted to use it to reveal Himself to His people, but Moses turned it into a circus sideshow to display his moral superiority. He robbed God of His glory.

That's why God then said to Moses and Aaron, "Because you did not trust in me enough to honor me as holy in the sight of the Israelites, you will not bring this community into the land I give them" (v. 12). Talk about a swift, severe punishment!

God is serious about the way we act. If we bear His image, then we should produce His actions.

Do you ever let your pride control your mouth
and actions? Has anyone made you angry by
disrespecting your rights or your authority?
Do you say things that may be true and right,
but not in a spirit of love and patience?
Do you do justice to God's image through
your words and deeds?
(See also James 1:19–21; 4:6–7.)

Christ Died for His Enemies

NOVEMBER 19, 2004

As you all know, we have begun the assault on Fallujah. I have sent a tank platoon there, and they are actually leading the charge into the assault. I have not heard much back on their progress other than that we have done amazingly well and my tanks are responsible for the deaths of over 60 insurgents.

We've had some rough going here in the wake of our assault on Fallujah. Insurgents have been packing vehicles with explosives in hopes of ramming a tank or Humvee and killing the soldiers inside. The other day I was conducting information-gathering operations from civilians in town when I got a call on my radio. One of my soldiers' tanks had just been rammed by an explosive-laden car, but the insurgent was knocked unconscious by the impact before the bombs detonated. One of the bombs had fallen out from under the car's hood. SSG Sheid, the tank commander, immediately shot the bomb and blew it up. However, there were five more bombs inside the car.

I arrived on the scene and started to analyze the vehicle. We saw wires coming from under the hood. The backseat was torn out, and I thought there might be more bombs in the trunk and backseat. I watched the driver carefully; my gunner had his machine gun trained on the insurgent's skull. I decided that this guy might be alive. No flies had gathered on his face, and his head had moved slightly as I watched.

I called for the bomb squad in hopes that we could defuse the bombs, pull the man from the car, and question him. The bomb squad arrived and stopped about a quarter mile from the vehicle. They dismounted their robot, whom we refer to affectionately as Johnny Five, with its camera eye and directed it to the bombsite. Through the robot's camera, we ascertained that the insurgent was in fact alive. Then the bomb squad turned Johnny Five's attention to the bomb, trying to understand how it was rigged. They decided that the only way to ensure our safety while pulling the man from the car was to use a block of C4 to blow up the initiator that was on the steering wheel.

The bomb squad brought the robot back to their Humvee, attached a piece of C4 to the robot, and then sent it back to the car. The bomb squad, using Johnny Five, carefully placed the C4 on the steering wheel and started the fuse. We battened all the tank's hatches and watched.

BOOM! The blast went off. Unfortunately, the explosion was larger than intended and caused the car to catch on fire. The intense heat woke the insurgent, and he started to roll away from the vehicle. He would roll once, then pass out, roll, and pass out. Then the car's gas tank blew and the rear of the vehicle was engulfed in flames. For a moment, I thought someone might be

able to run up to the vehicle and save the insurgent before the bombs exploded. However, I felt it was too risky. There was no way I was going to chance sacrificing one of my men or myself to save a man who tried to kill us, no matter what information he might have.

Moments later the fire ignited the bombs in the vehicle, setting off a massive explosion. I watched safely from my tank as the flames consumed the insurgent and everything in the vicinity. The car disintegrated.

When the smoke cleared, I dismounted the tank and ran to where the insurgent lay face down in the sand. His limbs had been ripped from his body. His face was buried in the sand, but he was still alive. His body convulsed as I watched him try to breathe, but the sand suffocated him. I watched the sand turn a deep red around him. Within seconds his body stopped trying to breathe and gave in to death. I almost felt sorry for him. We ran out of body bags so we took several trash bags and put his body in them. I reminded myself that this was the enemy, who had regarded me with nothing but pure contempt and malice and that he deserved to die.

I think he did deserve to die. The Bible says the wages of sin is death. But there was something more here and my mind continued to search for truth amongst such chaos.

A Scripture passage poured into my mind. "You see, at just the right time, when we were still powerless, Christ died for the ungodly. Very rarely will anyone die for a righteous man, though for a good man someone might possibly dare to die. But God demonstrates his own love for us in this: While we were still sinners, Christ died for us… When we were God's enemies, we were reconciled to him through the death of his Son" (Romans 5:6–8, 10).

Suddenly I saw myself in the corpse that lay before me. Before I came to Christ, I was that insurgent. By my very life I stood opposed to everything that God is. I was steeped in sin. Contemptuous. Malicious. I was ramming my proverbial car bomb into God, the Fortress. Of course, my efforts were useless, powerless. And for my efforts, I was about to be consumed by God's fire, when God the Son put Himself in my place. He pulled me from harm's way and dove into the flames, sacrificing His life that I might live.

Now I am no longer treated as an enemy, but as a son! That's the God we serve. I still find myself constantly ramming my car into God. Old habits die hard. And every time I sin, I find even those newest offenses forgiven, already punished when Christ took them on His own shoulders.

We forget so easily. Sometimes we revel in the demise of our enemies without giving thought to their souls. But we used to be the ones driving the car bomb. And God's amazing grace is meant for both us and them.

How about you? Do you realize that you were God's enemy, standing opposed to everything He is? Do you appreciate the love of Christ, that He died for you while you were still His enemy? How does this influence your attitude toward your own enemies? Do you pray for them? Are you willing to love them, even while they hate you?

My Tank Was Destroyed

November 23, 2004

The battle of Fallujah continues. Here at Camp Habbaniyah, we continue to work with limited combat power as I have a platoon of tanks at the tip of the spear ten miles away at Fallujah.

Here, things are slightly different, but the action is just as intense. Yesterday one of our tanks was almost hit by an insurgent. I decided it was time to take the fight to the enemy. I radioed battalion, informing them of my plan to go into uncharted territory in hopes of destroying some of the enemy's ambush capabilities. Then we set out.

We had ventured deep into the heart of an enemy-held residential area when I stopped and searched a suspicious-looking car. Via our radios, we submitted the occupants' names for screening through our database, and waited. It took forever. *With us stuck here, this would be a good time to set some kind of trap ahead of us,* I remember thinking.

We finally got confirmation that these men were clean. So I mounted my tank again and continued the patrol. As my tank and my wingman went around the corner, I noticed that there were not many people out. *Huh?*

BOOM! For a moment everything froze. Acrid-tasting black smoke billowed up around me. I saw flames shoot from underneath my tank's front left skirt. I felt the concussion as a double-stacked Chinese antitank mine lifted the left side of the seventy-two-ton tank into the air. Then we crashed down again. Unreal.

I ducked into the turret. In doing so, I skinned my shin—my only injury from the incident. SSG Burton stared wide-eyed back at me to see if I was injured. Or dead.

"I'm okay, I'm okay," I said. Sergeant Oates was safe as well.

"I'm okay," reported PFC Periani, my driver, over the intercom.

Suddenly the radio was ablaze with voices. My wingman called up frantically, saying that I had been hit by an IED. With as much calmness as I could muster I tried to radio in that I had been hit by an IED, but that I was okay. I called for maintenance support. Unfortunately my radios weren't strong enough, and no one could hear me. All they received were Don's frantic messages saying that my tank was blown to smithereens.

Which it was. The one-ton front left skirt was thrown two hundred feet from the tank, and the entire left side of the track was destroyed. I had been hit by IEDs before, but nothing like this. Before this, every tank damaged by an IED had rolled back to base under its own power.

I was out in the middle of nowhere. Granted, I had my wingman in a Bradley that could provide a hail of big bullets if an enemy got any crazy ideas. But I felt vulnerable. Helpless.

I got out and looked at the destruction. I was awed that no one inside had been injured. My driver looked at me and said that he now felt more comfortable in a tank than he ever had. In spite of the devastation to the track, nothing had penetrated the crew compartment.

A skeptic might look at this situation and say, "Wow, look at that obliterated tank. The insurgents got the upper hand. I thought the commander of this tank was a Christian. I wonder what he did to upset God."

But God Himself gives us a different perspective on this situation: "We know that in all things God works for the good of those who love him, who have been called according to his purpose" (Romans 8:28). So how in the world does this turn out good? It's not just four million bucks down the drain; it's a moral victory for the enemy. They destroyed a tank! Sure, I am alive, but if I have faith, then bad things shouldn't happen, right? Wrong!

Yes, this was a bad thing. But who am I to determine that the outcome will be bad as well? The truth that I have a hard time grasping is that I'm not the one who defines "good." God defines it. And if He is looking out for my good, then anything He causes or allows is the very best I could ever hope would happen in my life. In fact, when I'm all caught up in my own pity party, I can miss out on seeing and enjoying the good God wants to bring out of the situation. For if we focus on ourselves in the midst of moral defeat, humiliation, setbacks, then we cannot see the bigger picture.

In the military realm, the lesson here for my crew and me is to trust the tank. No matter what IED we encounter, we will always be okay if we're inside the tank.

Spiritually, the lesson for you and me is to trust God. He is impenetrable. He is completely aware of your situation, but nothing can ever budge His will off its sovereign track.

More than two and a half millennia ago, three men displayed this kind of confidence in God and His will. Their names were Shadrach, Meshach, and Abednego, and we read about them in Daniel 3. The Babylonian emperor Nebuchadnezzar had decreed that all his subjects must worship a huge statue of him. But these men obeyed God instead, who had commanded that we worship no one but Him. Because of their civil disobedience, they were about to be thrown into a furnace.

Were they scared? You bet. Did they plead for their lives? Nope. Instead they simply said, "O Nebuchadnezzar, we do not need to defend ourselves before you in this matter. If we are thrown into the blazing furnace, the God we serve is able to save us from it, and he will rescue us from your hand, O king. But even if he does not, we want you to know, O king, that we will not serve your gods or worship the image of gold you have set up" (3:16).

That's faith. God understands that our faith starts out weak. But in His wisdom, He allows us to encounter challenges that are appropriate to our maturity level. As we trust Him, His love, and His good plan in each situation, our faith grows stronger. And He gives us peace as we rest in Him.

As it turns out, Shadrach, Meshach, and Abednego were right. They were thrown into the furnace, but not a hair was singed. When they came out, their clothes didn't even smell like smoke. And Nebuchadnezzar himself had seen God, temporarily in human form, standing with His three servants in the flames (3:25). Just as He stood with me in my tank. Just as He will stand by you during your adversity.

*What are you going through right now that feels
like God's punishment? In what part of your
life do you need to let God define "good," rather
than determining your own definition? Do you
realize that God is with you, not against you? In
loneliness? In physical pain? In loss?*

Worship...Boring?

At church yesterday, I eagerly anticipated the baptism of SSG Falcon, the soldier I have been discipling. This was a new beginning for my soldier, and I wanted the experience to be just right. As I entered the chapel, with a full heart I greeted my friends from around the battalion who also attend Sunday worship. We began the service with a hymn.

Now, in many contemporary churches in the U.S., you get to worship with electric guitar, keyboard, drums, vocals, and PowerPoint or ProPresenter. Us? We have the chaplain standing in front, singing. That's it.

We sang "Oh, How He Loves You and Me." I noticed the dirt on the concrete floor. I also noticed that just about everyone was singing off key. Especially me. And for a moment my heart said, *This is not what I wanted here. This is not how baptisms are supposed to go. This is so...so boring.*

But it was only a moment. Because the next thing I felt was God's gentle vice grip of conviction on my heart. Immediately I knew I was wrong.

I had been thinking of this service from my perspective, and my heart was hardened. But like dawn creeping through the clouds, I began to see the worship service from God's perspective. Here were twenty or so men who daily band together as brothers to lay their lives down for their friends. Here are men who are not concerned about making an earthly show of worship. They're not here to impress people with their not-so-tuned voices or the dirty floor. They're here *to be impressed with God*, and to give Him their hearts. No pomp, just worship. Worship the way it was intended.

Through Amos, God told the Israelites that their worship was worthless. They used to overflow with love and reverence for Almighty God, but they had become hollow shells. God said, "I hate, I despise your religious feasts; I cannot stand your assemblies. Even though you bring me burnt offerings and grain offerings, I will not accept them. Though you bring choice fellowship offerings, I will have no regard for them. Away with the noise of your songs! I will not listen to the music of your harps. But let justice roll on like a river, righteousness like a never-failing stream!" (Amos 5:21–24).

God is pretty serious about the hearts of His people. He is not into the song if the heart of the singer is not in tune with Him. He is not pleased with the "high-techness" of the church if the focus of the church is not His glory. God is tired of people worshiping their own abilities or personal creativity. He's tired of people "worshiping" just to feel good. That isn't worship. And it means nothing to God.

In that moment in chapel, I could see it clearly. God is not so interested in what we do as in how we do it. This life is about Him and not about us. Not about me. How many times am I more worried about being entertained than worshiping a Holy God?

Is your worship focused on God? Or on yourself or your surroundings? Do you pay more attention to the ambience than to His glory? Are you disappointed when your favorite song is not played? Are you bored when you sing an old hymn? Are you critical of simple sermons? Are you more interested in being entertained than worshiping God? Evaluate your heart and be honest before Him.

Sigh

Some days are worse than others, but today was particularly tough. It started when the screeching radios woke me at 0836. Two Humvees were patrolling a hot area when the lead Humvee hit an antitank mine similar to the one that destroyed my tank. If an IED can destroy a tank, you can imagine what it did to the Humvee. It caused the Humvee to flip forward once in the air and then to somersault two more times along the ground. The driver and the truck commander were thrown through the roof and were caught between the roof and the windshield as the Humvee flipped end over end. Two great Americans dead. Two loving families with broken hearts after a visit from a chaplain and a casualty assistance officer.

I went to church yesterday morning and my heart was low. We sang, the chaplain spoke, and my mind was on the battle. *More dead.* I sighed. *Lord, how much more can we take?*

I returned to my tactical operations center and listened to the radios.

"IED, IED!"

Not again.

Then the three letters that break the heart of any soldier: *KIA.*

My heart sank another foot. I let out a defeated sigh.

I took my tank and the Bradley out on patrol in sector. The streets were stark, not a soul out.

The soldiers who died were not in my company, but it al-

114

most felt as if they were. I couldn't shake off a deep sense of loss. I visited the battalion operations center where the colonel and a lieutenant wept unabashedly, sharing the burden of grief. I did a lot of looking at my boots. And heaved a heavy sigh.

I was given a mission. A particular house had been used as a platform for sniper fire. I was to raid the house and question those inside. I took the concept of the operation from the Battalion Operations Officer and discussed it with my leaders. That night we conducted the raid and found nothing. We had to take the owner in for further questioning. As so often before, I endured the hateful looks from children as their father was taken away, the screams of a wife as we pried her fingers off of her husband's arms.

Lord, I hate this.

Even though I knew we would release the husband in a couple of hours, there was no way for the woman and children to understand. Another deep sigh.

Sometimes I feel the weight of the world on my shoulders. Everything seems to be falling apart around me. I wonder

whether God truly understands my pain. He is God, but can He really comprehend frustration? If He wanted to, He could just fix it, and there would be no more death and no more tearing families apart.

No more sighs.

Back in my quarters I took off my body armor and boots and sat down on my cot beneath my mosquito net. I opened my Bible to Mark 7. If you like to skim your Bible like I do, then you will miss it. But this time I was ready to see it. "There some people brought to [Jesus] a man who was deaf and could hardly talk, and they begged him to place his hand on the man. After he took him aside, away from the crowd, Jesus put his fingers into the man's ears. Then he spit and touched the man's tongue. He looked up to heaven and *with a deep sigh* said to him, 'Ephphatha!' (which means, 'Be opened!'). At this, the man's ears were opened, his tongue was loosened and he began to speak plainly" (vv. 32–35, emphasis mine).

Did you see it? Jesus sighed. Deeply. He had seen disbelief, He had seen heartache, people were missing the point. He tried to get some time alone, but the crowd always tracked Him down, not because they wanted to worship Him, but because they wanted the miracles He could perform. He sighed.

I read on through chapter 8. Jesus fed the multitudes and continued to prove His identity through miracles. Then "the Pharisees came and began to question Jesus. To test him, they asked him for a sign from heaven. *He sighed deeply* and said, 'Why does this generation ask for a miraculous sign? I tell you the truth, no sign will be given to it.' Then he left them, got back into the boat and crossed to the other side" (vv. 11–13). If feeding several thousand people with a few loaves and fish wasn't a sign, what would they possibly accept?

Jesus was tired. He was tired of people seeing the hand of God and totally not getting it. He was frustrated because He loved so deeply and did not receive that love in return.

I realized then that God did understand. The writer of Hebrews was right: "We do not have a high priest who is unable to sympathize with our weaknesses, but we have one [Jesus] who has been tempted in every way, just as we are—yet was without sin. Let us then approach the throne of grace with confidence, so that we may receive mercy and find grace to help us in our time of need" (Hebrews 4:15–16).

I can approach God with the burdens of the world and give them to Him. He is not only aware of what is going on, but He has been through it Himself. Like a battle-weary warrior, He knows my troubles. Like an exasperated mother who cares for me, He knows my heart. Like the persecuted, He knows injustice and sorrow. He knows the burdens you're carrying. He knows your tears.

Even when we're dealing with something as heavy as death—*especially* then—we can approach the throne of grace with confidence; we will find mercy and grace in our time of need.

*What burdens are you carrying today? What
tears have you shed? Have you sighed today?
Do you need a little mercy? A little grace?
A little hope?*

Your God knows what it is to sigh.

Leftovers Again?

DECEMBER 13, 2004

The Internet has been down for a month, and amid the pain and agony here, it's a great relief to have it back. For a while it felt like we were cut off from the outside world. Now my men are talking to their families regularly, and I also get to chat with my family and pretty much anyone else who hops online.

But today I realized that I have been overindulging in Internet chat. It seems that every waking minute I'm not actively involved in a battle, there's somebody online that I have to talk to. The Internet in and of itself is not a bad thing. But while our access was down, I spent hours with God each day, reading His Word, reading a Christian book (I read four or five during the "Web fast"), or teaching anyone who was around me about our amazing God.

I'm amazed to see how my prayer time shrank and how my Bible reading dwindled. When I finish chatting, I'm just too tired to focus my energy on God, and I always promise to do it in the morning. But when morning comes, there's someone else I want to talk to online. And all of a sudden God is getting my leftovers. And the way I've been going, there hasn't been much left over. I didn't realize until today how dry my soul has been feeling.

We easily fall into the mindset that we are too busy for God. We say things like, "I just don't have time for God. I know that God is good and all, but let's be pragmatic here. I can't just set aside my life for a God I can't see."

When I start thinking clearly, these excuses are replaced with a new thought: *God owns time.* But even though time belongs to Him, He gives us freedom to choose our priorities.

Moses, in Psalm 90:12, said, "Teach us to number our days aright, that we may gain a heart of wisdom." Moses longed for God to instruct him and his people in the art of eternally focused, God-centered time management. He wanted to think rightly about what was important.

During times of smooth sailing, we can become complacent and allocate time to everything but God. But I'm amazed how we often reorder our lives in the face of crisis, when reality drops some bomb on our lives. All of a sudden everything becomes clear and we realize that God is worthy of better than we've been giving Him.

After a heart attack, many people are suddenly able to find time for God. Prayer ceases to be just a church thing; it becomes a life constant.

When a woman threatens to leave with the kids, suddenly

the husband finds time to talk to God and to his family.

If a doctor gave us one month to live, we would find ourselves face to face with eternity. We would be much more likely to reorder our lives to make everything count for God, to live life as vibrantly as possible. Well, guess what? The Doctor (the Great Physician) has issued His prognosis. Your condition is 100-percent fatal. You have only one life to live. What a concept.

Jesus observed people and their amazing capacity for worry. Worry about food. Worry about clothes. Worry about money for the house payment. Worry about keeping up with the next guy. Worry about fitting in. Worry about missing out. Worry about our own significance in the big picture. *Will my life really amount to anything?*

And pursuing their own answers keeps people very, very busy.

So in the middle of the Sermon on the Mount, Jesus explained how simple God's agenda really is: "Seek first his kingdom and his righteousness, and all these things will be given to you as well" (Matthew 6:33).

When you seek God's righteousness and not your own selfishness, when you put God's kingdom ahead of your personal "sovereignty"—you will find that things slow down just a bit. You begin to see all of the other things, which seemed so important, as just more busy work. And you find ways of making God the center of your schedule, and fitting everything else in around Him.

Are you all wrapped up in doing, doing, doing?
Are you so consumed with being all things to all
people that your relationship with the One who
is all things to you is slipping? What priorities
do you need to reorder? How do you need to
number your days aright? What things do you
need to cut out so that God gets your first fruits
and not your leftovers?

A Shot in the Armor

DECEMBER 20, 2004

Yesterday I received a call from one of my tank commanders, reporting something suspicious in the area he was patrolling. He observed a lot of expensive cars converging on one house, and he thought it might be a terrorist cell meeting. That was good enough for me, so I mounted my metal steed and headed on into the fray. I gathered some of my men, and we conducted a thorough search of the area. We interviewed various suspects and received the usual response: "We know nothing. We are a peaceful people." As so often before, we once again came up empty. Nonetheless something was definitely awry.

I headed back to base, and as soon as I returned to my tactical operations center, I received a call on the radio from that same tank commander saying that he had just taken sniper fire. His loader was hit. The loader fell into the turret of the tank. The first reaction to enemy contact is always to return fire, which the tank commander did. Then once the smoke cleared, he checked on his loader. His arm hurt a little from falling into the turret, but there was no blood. The tank commander inspected the loader's body armor. There was a hole in the outer fabric, but no penetration of the plates. The armor stopped the bullet. A 7.62-mm round was found crumpled at the base of the armor. The sniper had been foiled this time.

This happened only because my soldier was properly dressed and equipped. The loader was not planning on getting shot yesterday. It was not something he woke up thinking about. He put on his armor because only a fool would leave the safety of our base without it. He also put it on because his tank commander, SFC Stemen—a responsible man of wisdom and experience—would never let him go out into sector without protection.

Yet I wonder how many of us fail to put on our spiritual body armor daily. How often do we venture out "into sector" in the seemingly safe world of everyday life, foolishly ignoring the danger of satanic sniper fire?

In Ephesians 6:11–12, Paul exhorts us to "put on the full armor of God so that you can take your stand against the devil's schemes. For our struggle is not against flesh and blood, but against the rulers, against the authorities, against the powers of this dark world and against spiritual forces of evil in the heavenly realms."

This is military talk, because we're all soldiers, and we all live on a battlefield. Paul continues on to describe our spiritual armor: truth, righteousness, readiness for the gospel, faith, understanding of our salvation, and the ability to use the Word of God. These are what soldiers of the cross must "put on" in order to fight an enemy that we cannot see. When we don't put it on, we're susceptible to Satan's traps.

As we say here in Iraq, "Complacency kills." True in Iraq, true in life. It isn't "just because" that pride or lust trips me up. It isn't "just because" that my temper trips me up over and over. It isn't "just because" that I sin. When I don't purposefully, consciously armor up with God, I am a sitting duck for Satan.

Okay, okay. I can hear you. You're saying, "That briefs well and makes a pretty devotional, but how do you put on truth? Where do I go to get some righteousness? How about faith? You know where I can get some of that?"

In a word, yes. Have you ever noticed that the Bible never calls us to fight as Lone Rangers? Yet our American, independent spirit, which has forged an amazing freedom, can also lead us to think that we can achieve victory alone. Paul knew better. He was coaching a young pastor named Titus about how believers in the church needed to help each other dress for battle. One of his key strategies was to direct older men and women to mentor younger men and women, modeling godly attitudes and actions for them. And to Titus himself, Paul said, "In everything set them an example by doing what is good. In your teaching show integrity, seriousness and soundness of speech that cannot be condemned" (Titus 2:7–8). Just as a tank commander would never let one of his men go into sector without his body armor, so we should care enough for each other to equip each other spiritually for daily spiritual warfare.

Spiritual armor doesn't just happen. People don't just wake up and figure out how to be faithful. Gaining maturity in your faith is an ongoing process. What we need is men and women who will rise up and offer experience and leadership to others. And we all must come under another's spiritual authority, for our own safety, and for God's victory. We need each other's help to get through the difficult times in our marriages, to overcome pride or lust. We need to work together to quell dissension in our churches. We need to equip each other to stay strong through life transitions, to be ready to lead that neighbor, friend, or family member to Christ.

For those who are younger reading this, find an example and ask them to mentor you. For those who are older, find someone younger in the faith and show them what you know.

How well-equipped are you for everyday
warfare? Who can you invite to help you learn to
put on God's armor and to use it properly?
Who else can you help do this?

Depravity of Man

I had another day of tough action out in sector. An enemy sniper stealthily slipped in behind a house and prepared to shoot at one of my observation posts. But one of my own snipers spotted him first. My man carefully took aim and shot. Radios barked loudly. Everyone converged on the scene. My tank moved around the houses while I scanned nooks and crannies with my ten-power optics. Nothing.

My sniper was sure he had hit the guy. But apparently the enemy rescued their casualty and pulled him somewhere safe before we could find him. We searched and searched and found nothing. Frustration started to build. But our attention was quickly redirected when the radio sparked up.

"Apache 6, this is Reaper 3. I have a truck with four dead men heading east."

"Roger."

I told my driver to kick it in gear because we needed to get to that vehicle. The turbine engine whirred, and soon we were moving our depleted-uranium behemoth at top speed.

I soon came upon one of the most horrifying sights I've yet seen here. Four sets of feet protruded from the back of a pickup truck. In the United States someone might create something that looked like this, sticking out of their trunk as a practical joke. This was no joke. I approached to find four men with bullet holes in their heads and handcuffs cinched tightly around their wrists.

Four Iraqi men murdered for wanting their country to be free, executed at pointblank range. They were stacked like cordwood in the truck bed. I gripped the dead man on top and grimaced. Rigor mortis had set in. He wore a veil of blood that had now dried over his face. His arms could not be bent. My heart sank as I saw a chipped piece of skull fall from his head. He had been shot through the mouth and through the brain.

Blood...brains...skull. Dear God.

In the aftermath of something like this, lots of eyebrows are raised. *God, how could You let this happen? What is going on with this world? Why are people killing each other without regard?*

Clearly something is inherently wrong with this world, and the depravity of man becomes obvious. In some way it's a part of every day of our lives. Maybe you don't see evil as grotesquely displayed as it was for me, but it is there. Maybe you've seen someone cheat...just a little bit here and there. Maybe you've heard someone speak a little falsehood. Christians do it as well. I know; I'm one of them. We are all susceptible to the sinful tendencies of human nature. It is not merely non-Christians who run after their own desires. Since the fall of man, we have all been prone to blood lust.

A long time ago a man committed a simple, small sin. He ate from a tree from which he was told not to eat, causing this human condition we call the depravity of man. "Therefore...sin entered the world through one man, and death through sin, and in this way death came to all men, because all sinned" (Romans 5:12).

Among Adam's offspring we see sin reigning unchecked, from the first murder (of Abel by Cain) to these four Iraqi citizens murdered by terrorists. Sin reigns unchecked in an individual, murderous sniper who might have had me in his sight just yesterday, and might again tomorrow. It all becomes both very global and very personal, and a cloud of despair looms low over the languid heart as we dare to think on such things.

We find ourselves in a flawed world. There is no one good. This is the stuff that causes some Christians to turn to atheism and confirms atheists in their conclusions. If God is so great and good, then why all this evil in His world?

I don't claim to know the full answer to that question, but one thing I do know. In Romans 5, Paul continues with a note of hope. *The* hope. The mother of all hopes. The hope to end all despair. "Just as the result of one trespass was condemnation for all men, so also the result of one act of righteousness was justification that brings life for all men. For just as through the disobedience of the one man [Adam] the many were made sinners, so also through the obedience of the one man [Jesus] the many will be made righteous" (vv. 18–19).

As I write this, we're entering the season when we celebrate the birth of Jesus Christ. The birth of the Savior of the world. I wonder if we truly realize what Christ has saved us from—the depravity of man. We saw it recently when a man blew himself up in a mess tent in Mosul, a hundred miles from here. We just saw it when four men were executed for trying to give freedom to their country. I saw it while trying to hunt down a man with a gun, who wanted to hunt down one of us first.

You see it when you speak a little lie to cover up laziness. You see it when you skim a little off the top; who's going to notice? You see it when people cheat on their spouses. Depravity surrounds us. And it inhabits us.

But God provides hope. A cure for sin. A Son. A Savior.

Where do you see the depravity of man around you? In you? Do you recognize your need for the Savior? Do you understand why He was born? Have you received His gift of salvation, forgiveness, life?

Tanking = Praying

One of the unique things about a tank crew is that each of us speaks to the others by means of a headset that is known as a "combat vehicle crewman's helmet." We call it a CVC for short. The only time that you cannot hear each other is when someone becomes disconnected from the "J-box"—that is, the junction box, into which we all plug our CVCs.

Of course, communication is critically important during combat operations, during which the talk is all high excitement—gun battles, car chases, and arresting bad guys. But some days life in sector is exceedingly boring, so we sit around and talk. Traditionally at these times, soldiers fall back on four topics: fornication, intoxication, defecation, and God. I like to think that my crew supersedes this repertoire.

I love working together with this system of communication; it's like one mind with four different thinkers. This system is critical to our survival, because as a crew we must become so cohesive as to act as one. Indeed, this is exactly what happens in a crew that has been together for a while. In fact, a good tank crew becomes so unified that words are sometimes unnecessary for their coordinated action.

The other day we were going out into sector, and all I had to tell Mendez, my driver, was "D Sector." He knew right where to go. As we drove, we were about to come to a part of the road where I like to drive against traffic, because driving randomly makes it hard for the enemy to predict our movements. (Besides, when else can I drive forty miles per hour against sixty-mile-per-hour oncoming traffic?)

"Now, sir?" asked Mendez.

"Roger."

With no further explanation, Mendez switched to the other side of the highway, just as I wished. It was awesome.

On the way back, I started to explain that I wanted him to cross the median to go against traffic again. Now, it's not safe to cross the median just anywhere, because soft dirt may hide mines. So looking through my periscopes, I saw ahead where I wanted Mendez to turn.

"Hey, ahh…" I paused trying to think of how to describe the exact location.

"Roger, sir, I got it."

No need to explain. We had been together so long that our coordinated action was second nature.

It was not like that at first. We went through several exasperating trials. "Left, left, steady on. Wait. Right, right, right… okay, there." That was painful. But after a couple of months I would just grunt something, and he would understand exactly what I was talking about. That freed me to my other units on the battlefield while he took me exactly where I wanted to go.

Our communion with God starts out very much the same way. It's hard going at the beginning, because we're just getting acquainted. It may feel like our prayers are hitting the ceiling, or like we have to reintroduce ourselves to God every time we pray. *Dear God, this is Jimmy. I just met you last week and would like to say hey.*

Later on, prayer can become a meaningless ritual. We go to a certain place, we mention all of the usual issues, then we sign off. Amen. *By the way, God, if you need me, I'll be watching the*

Super Bowl. You can holler at me during a commercial. Just make sure it's not a funny one. And that's about it.

What Jesus wants, though, is that our prayer life become much more intimate than:

1. *Dear God…*
2. *List of stuff.*
3. *Amen.*

He wants prayer to be an experience of constant commnication. Like riding in your tank all day long with God and listening to His guidance as he leads you on the spiritual battlefield.

Some days you will pause and just sit with Him and jaw about life. Other times it will be high adventure, and you will be operating on one-word cues from Him. And sometimes, when you have to work your way through an especially tight spot, there will be a lot of "left, left, left, steady, right, right, rights."

But the theme that runs through it all is *constant communication*. Keeping your CVC plugged into the J-box is essential, or else you will have no idea what He wants to tell you.

That's what Paul was talking about when he instructed us to "pray continually" (1 Thessalonians 5:17). Continual prayer isn't sitting on your knees all day, or stumbling around with your eyes closed. It's walking through every moment of life aware that Jesus is your driver and your companion. He's sitting next to you on the ride to work. He's looking over your shoulder as you crunch out stupid government-required paperwork late on a Friday evening.

With God, you can use as many or as few words as the moment requires. He already knows what you need. And even better than that, He has the ability and desire to give it to you.

Is something keeping you from staying in constant communication with your Provider? How can you invite Him to break down the barrier? Do you believe that He listens, cares, and can give you the guidance you need? If not, then remember: The more time you spend with Him, the better you'll trust Him.

Christmas in Iraq

DECEMBER 25, 2004

Ahhh, the Christmas season. A time when families gather to celebrate. But for those of us in Iraq, it has been a little different. A globe lies between us and our loved ones, and Christmas trees are decorated at home in our absence. Instead of opening presents with his kids, a father waits in line for the next available phone. Instead of an eighteen-year-old hanging out with Mom, Dad, and the folks, he sits on his cot and plays a video game.

Add to that loneliness the cold, blustery weather of an Iraqi winter, and it combines to form a gloom that weighs the heart of even the happiest of campers.

What a lot of my men did not know was that Virginia Cook Realtors in Dallas, Texas, had made it their personal mission to bring a little home over to us in Iraq. Seventy boxes containing everything from basketballs to peanut butter and jelly to wet wipes filled our dayroom. On Christmas morning I asked the men to assemble in the dayroom. They filed in, some still groggy, others still dressed in all their gear, fresh back out of sector. Virtually all of them were unengaged, disinterested, apathetic. This was not where they wanted to be for Christmas.

I loved watching as they walked in and saw the mountain of gifts. Looks of awe and disbelief came over their faces. Before we dug in, I grouped them all together for a picture. We prayed. We talked about our fallen comrades and smiled, remembering how one was always talking about Jesus, the other bragging that he was an actual porn star.

Then we dove in with a flurry of ribbon-snipping and paper-ripping. We joked. Behaved like boys.

Behaved like family.

I stood back at one point and watched my men interacting as brothers, forgetting the troubles of battle, forgetting the heartache of missing home. Men together. A Band of Brothers.

Some were loaders. Some tank commanders. Some gunners. Some tank drivers. Supply soldiers, mechanics, medics, artillerymen, infantrymen. And presiding over the unit was the father figure offering his wisdom, my first sergeant, senior enlisted man in the company.

We each have our roles. In battle every man counts. No man is unimportant. Anytime someone gets hurt it affects the entire company. The entire company feels the effects of discord. And especially in the event of a death, the entire company feels the loss. We have many parts, but we function as one. We have a common cause. Sometimes painful discipline must be enforced, but it saves lives. Everyone is a valuable part. We have no spares.

Some people at home in the U.S. may think that we rally around the flag, Mom, and apple pie. Those are all important to us, but in war, when we fight, we fight for the man to our left and the soldier to our right.

Christians are all part of one family. One unit in warfare. Our cause is to love the Lord our God with all our heart, mind, soul, and strength. The primary way we do that is by looking out for the man or woman to our left, the soldier to our right. We all have different roles in the body of Christ, but each member is critically important. And we glorify Him by loving each other as parts of one body.

Paul puts it like this: "It was [Christ] who gave some to be apostles, some to be prophets, some to be evangelists, and some to be pastors and teachers, to prepare God's people for works of service, so that the body of Christ may be built up until we all reach unity in the faith and in the knowledge of the Son of God and become mature, attaining to the whole measure of the fullness of Christ" (Ephesians 4:11–13).

Paul is clear about what happens when we come together as one instead of living in disunity: "Then we will no longer be infants…. Instead, speaking the truth in love, we will in all things grow up into him who is the Head, that is, Christ. From him the whole body, joined and held together by every supporting ligament, grows and builds itself up in love, as each part does its work" (vv. 14–16).

That's not just a pipe dream. It can become reality. But we must submit ourselves wholly to the body of Christ. The church is made up of everyone working together to push toward Christ with ever-increasing vigor. That is the quest of the body. Some will be tempted to step aside or quit because the going gets tough. Let's encourage each other to do our part, no matter what it may be. Every person matters within the body of Christ.

Do you feel that you are not an important part of the body of Christ? Do you live your life as a team player or as a lone ranger? Are you allowing the body to discipline you and mature you in the faith? Have you lost confidence in the church and want nothing to do with it? How could you pursue healing from God and from people?

As a Soldier Craves Pizza...

JANUARY 7, 2005

This week I went to the American Embassy in Baghdad. I met with an Air Force lawyer who will be the prosecuting attorney for an insurgent who fired an RPG at one of my gun trucks. I arrived by helicopter at the embassy building, which used to be one of Saddam's palaces. "Huge" and "opulent" don't even begin to describe this place. I left Camp Habbaniyah without much time to pack and my uniform was very dirty. I looked like I had just come straight from the battlefield. Basically because...I had. I could feel the stares as I walked through the building, passing dozens of starched uniforms and never-fired weapons.

When I arrived at the lawyer's office, a wide-eyed captain accosted me and wanted me to tell him "the stories." In the embassy the greatest danger was that of a very sharp sheet of paper slicing an unlucky finger.

We went to meet with an Iraqi judge, and through an interpreter I presented the evidence against the RPG man. We had a very solid case against him—two eyewitnesses confirming his attempt to kill my soldier. When we finished, I was dismissed and escorted back to my quarters. That was easy. Now it was time to enjoy Baghdad.

One of the main attractions of Baghdad was Pizza Inn. I ordered, and a few minutes later took my first bite of pizza in...well, um, a long time. For a moment I was transported back to Texas. (I know Chicago and New York are where real pizza is made, but I am from Texas, so that's where I was transported.) It was amazing.

Then the lightbulb popped up. *This is something my men would enjoy.* I bought a cooler and ordered six pizzas to go. I packed other items in the cooler so the pizzas would not bounce around in the helicopter too badly. Then I waited and finally boarded the aircraft.

Upon arrival at my base, I was greeted by my executive officer and first sergeant. They said they were happy to see me, and briefed me on the events I had missed. Then their eyes took in something they were even happier to see.

"Pizza?"

I grinned and nodded. "Pizza."

"Pizza!"

People scampered around, spreading the amazing news. Although it was 2:30 a.m., soldiers walked in sleepy-eyed to get a taste of a treat they had not enjoyed in a long, long time. Even if they got only one slice, it brought them immense joy.

I watched for a moment and thought of how I longed for a quiet time with the Lord. An odd thing to think at a moment like that? You have to understand that here "alone" time is very hard to come by. Radios squawking nonstop twenty feet from my bed. People walking into my room all the time to ask advice, receive orders, request my signature. I stood watching all of my consumers of pizza, and what I longed to taste was some time alone with God.

Then I realized that the time is always there, if I make it. And making the "sacrifice" for time with God is what fills my soul. We all struggle with this. We are all busy, all so pressed for time, all so rushed.

But as a soldier craves pizza, so my soul craves You, O God.

That's my modern paraphrase of David's words in Psalm 42: "As the deer pants for streams of water, so my soul pants for you, O God. My soul thirsts for God, for the living God. When can I go and meet with God?" (vv. 1–2).

I was living these words. Even though this was a moment of happiness and contentment with my men, my soul felt somehow downcast. Needing a taste of God. Drink of the Divine.

That's exactly how David felt: "Why are you downcast, O my soul? Why so disturbed within me? Put your hope in God, for I will yet praise him, my Savior and my God" (vv. 5–6).

We're designed with a need to return regularly to our Source of life. When we are down, when the walls of life are closing in, when there is no other place to turn. When you feel like giving up on the whole thing, when those who are supposed to love you have turned their backs on you, when you feel cheated, when you feel hurt, when the decisions you have hurriedly made start to backfire, when you are at the end of the rope…

Put your hope in God. Drink from Him. Bathe in His praise.

When was the last "meal" you had with God? How can you plan regular "feedings" into your week? Thank Him now for building into you that craving that only He can satisfy.

This Conversation Is Over!

Another week has passed here in Iraq, and the challenges continue.

"Apache Tango! Apache Tango! This is Blue 2…" The soldier's voice was high-pitched with excitement. I ran to the radios to see what this was about. Another casualty? An IED?

"Blue 2, this is Apache 6! What is going on?" No answer. I turned to one of my soldiers. "Get the QRF (quick reaction force). Let's go!" I wasn't sure what was happening, but it did not sound good.

"Apache 6, this is Blue 2. I engaged a man emplacing an IED. We did not hit him. He is heading into the town. I need infantry support to go after him."

I radioed to my infantry to move down to the location. They had heard the original call and were already sweeping the area.

Blue 2's voice became a lot calmer. "Apache 6, Blue 2. I think the guy got away."

"This is Apache 6, roger. Continue to monitor the area and keep me informed."

"Roger."

"Roger, out."

Though it wasn't the outcome we might hope for, this situation was now handled. I went outside to let the tank and the Bradley crews stand down. The gunner from my tank was filling in for SSG Burton. I told him to stand down.

He looked back at me, and I was surprised to find myself the target of an explosive round of frustration. "Sir, where are my guys at? Where are my guys at?"

I have never before received such disrespect from one of my men. Synapses zapped in my brain, and I went from relaxed to cutthroat in less than a second.

"What!? Get up here sergeant!" I screamed. He obeyed at top speed and stood at attention. "Don't you ever ask me where your men are! That is your responsibility. Do you understand me?"

He tried to respond, but I cut him off. "This conversation is over!" And I walked away. I knew without asking that I had made him feel really small.

Now, you must also know that this sergeant is a good leader and an amazing Christian. This was his first day gunning for me, and he wasn't used to controlling a quick reaction force. So he was already stressed out. What is more, the reason his men were missing was that another sergeant had taken the QRF tank crew to chow at the mess hall. That is a big no-no.

However, neither my gunner nor I knew that, so the confusion wasn't due to my gunner's irresponsibility, but that of the other sergeant. So in the end, my gunner took my full wrath for something that was not his fault.

Nonetheless, I rationalized that I was in the right. I am the commander. A sergeant should know where his soldiers are.

Over the next several days, every time I went to prayer, I felt a pounding on my heart. God brought to mind Job 32:13–14: "If I have denied justice to my menservants and maidservants when they had a grievance against me, what will I do when God confronts me? What will I answer when called to account?"

I could feel Him calling me to account. But, I kept trying

to tell God, I have the right to talk to anyone any way I want. *I make the law here. I am the commander.*

Okay. I could sense God's reply. *I'll give you that technicality. But if you want to argue technicalities…* And He reminded me of Jesus' confrontation with the legalists in Matthew 23:23: "Woe to you, teachers of the law and Pharisees, you hypocrites! You give a tenth of your spices—mint, dill and cummin. But you have neglected the more important matters of the law—justice, mercy and faithfulness. You should have practiced the latter, without neglecting the former."

The verse that pierced my heart and kept hitting me in the head was Matthew 5:23–24: "If you are offering your gift at the altar and there remember that your brother has something

against you, leave your gift there in front of the altar. First go and be reconciled to your brother; then come and offer your gift."

I knew my brother had something against me. I knew that his heart was hurting. Every time I went to God to pray, this issue would arise. There was nothing else to do but be reconciled. So with a humble heart, I called the sergeant into my room and we sat down together. I explained why I was upset, and I asked him to forgive me for yelling and for being hard of heart. He smiled and we prayed. My shoulders felt fifty pounds lighter. It was awesome. All the barriers were gone.

Upon leaving he said, "I knew you would do the right thing."

Humility consumed me. I felt complete. It's funny how God is always right.

I hope you're seeking an intimate relationship with God. If you're like me, it's easy to let relational rifts deepen with those around you. In our pride, we have a hard time letting go of the wrong of the other person. And that keeps us from admitting our own contribution to the problem.

Even if you are 95-percent right, you are still 5-percent wrong. You'll go a long way toward reconciliation by acknowledging your part and asking forgiveness for it, no matter whether the other party accepts any blame or not. If you do this, you may only be 5-percent wrong, but you're willingly and wisely taking 100-percent responsibility for mending the rift.

Accept the blame for your part of the wrong. And even more importantly, rise up, be the bigger person, and take full responsibility for fixing the problem. That's maturity.

Is there anyone to whom you need to admit you are wrong (without pointing out the wrong of the other)? How can you get your pride out of the way? Does your "brother" have something against you? What action do you need to take to make it right?

The Delegation

JANUARY 16, 2005

Remember the scene in *Braveheart* where the two armies are lined up opposite each other, a wide no-man's land between them? That's what I thought of as I dismounted my tank and walked out into the space between my troops and the 1200-strong line of Iraqi demonstrators in front of the mosque in the town of Husebah. They carried banners reading, "We want freedom," "We want water and other services," "No to Violence, Yes to Peace."

With me, cautiously walked my interpreter and a personal security detachment. The town elders approached from the other direction. Cautiously. So far, so good. I fingered my trigger and was thankful for my sunglasses. They made me look tough. I quickly scanned the rooftops for possible enemy snipers. Then I stopped and eyed the Iraqi delegation.

They were wearing the traditional Muslim one-piece robe, called a *dish-dasha*. My men call it a man-dress. They greeted me with the customary handshake and touch of the heart. The elders proceeded to communicate their demands through my translator. They wanted back all the people we had arrested. They wanted us to stop shooting without reason. And more, a whole list. Some of their demands were reasonable—like opening up a gas station. Others weren't—like sending all of our soldiers home.

I explained that the people we arrested were arrested for a reason. Multiple sources had identified them as the ones emplacing IEDs on the roads. I explained that we also fired our guns for a reason; when people shoot RPGs, rifles, or rockets at us, we will return fire. Sometimes we shoot at the IEDs in the ground to protect their children from getting blown up. (It has happened.) I affirmed that I loved them as my brothers and that I wanted peace. But they must help us, not turn a blind eye when a terrorist plants a bomb in front of their shop or house.

It was an exhilarating moment. I promised we would do everything within our power to help them. But until the terrorists left and there was peace in the streets, we would be forced to stay. And we would not hide. I told them we were not afraid to face the terrorists every day, as long as it took.

Then I said, "It brings tears to my eyes to think of the innocent people and especially the children who have been hurt here. I am truly saddened by it, and I long to make it right." We shared a moment of compassion as we talked of my men who had died, and their people who had died, as a result of war. We then shook hands, and they released the crowd. It was incredibly peaceful. Sometimes diplomacy works. I took their list of complaints, and the incident was over.

Here's the interesting thing to me. I had no orders stating specifically that I would be the one to mediate between the civilian delegation and U.S. forces, but nonetheless I ended up right there in the middle of it. I was the sole spokesman for the United States. It wasn't planned; it just happened. I was guided by what I knew my commander wanted, what I knew he would tell these people. It wasn't hard; I had spent a lot of time with him and had listened as he explained his heart, how he wanted justice for the Iraqis. In a sense, he helped form my words. I had absorbed them through verbal osmosis.

Peter wrote to Christians in his day, "Always be prepared to give an answer to everyone who asks you to give the reason for the hope that you have. But do this with gentleness and respect, keeping a clear conscience, so that those who speak maliciously against your good behavior in Christ may be ashamed of their slander" (1 Peter 3:15–16).

I wasn't specifically ordered to represent the U.S. to the Iraqis, but I had to be prepared to speak on behalf of the United States. All of us as followers of Christ are ordered to represent God's kingdom to the world. It is our calling to "go and make disciples of all nations, baptizing them in the name of the Father and of the Son and of the Holy Spirit, and teaching them to obey everything I have commanded you" (Matthew 28:19–20). Too often we expect that someone else is going to do it, and we can become lax in our learning and in our ability to give a reason for the hope that we have.

How do you know what to say? What is the reason for your hope? You spend a lot of time listening to your Commander, Jesus Christ. His heart and mind have been revealed in the Word of God. He expects us to become fully briefed with His truth, in order that we might skillfully answer those who don't know. People wandering in a fog, desperate for direction. People begging for freedom.

Are you prepared? Can you explain your hope,
why you believe, and what you believe? Can
you show the way to Christ's freedom? Are
you genuinely concerned for the plight of lost
people? Do you really believe your own message?
How will you ensure adequate time with your
Commander? Who will you love with His truth?

First Love

There I was, conducting another snatch and grab. The informant we were picking up was a Kurd who had been abused by the Baath party and was now looking forward to elections in a couple of weeks. He had just been ousted from Fallujah and was living near our base. He had no tolerance for terrorists. His brother had just been injured by a bomb, and a couple of kids were killed. This man was more than willing to come in and talk to us. He asked us to arrest him so that he would not be thought of as a source for us. So here we were arresting him.

When we entered his house, we found him tending to his brother's wounds. The women of the family were dressed in mostly western-style clothes. This was crazy. This was the first time I had seen an Iraqi woman wearing jeans.

I was stunned when I saw one young woman. She had soft almond eyes and high cheekbones, and a slender figure. She was simply beautiful, and she spoke impeccable English. This was quite the rarity.

She treated us like heroes, staring at us with unmitigated awe. To her, we were bringers of freedom. To her, we were her saviors. I have received many e-mails and cards from people in the States saying "Thank you," and "God bless you," and "You are a hero." But this girl broadcasted one clear, unprecedented message: *Wow!*

While my medic tended to her father, she bombarded me

151

with questions. Where was I from? How old was I? Was I married? She was ready to walk the aisle right then and there.

She kept touching my clothes and grabbing at my hands to see if I was real. I blushed. Muhammed, my interpreter, laughed at me. "What's up, sir? Your face become red?" he chided.

I left that house with a huge smile on my face. One of my soldiers walked up to me. "Sir, you can't smile like that. It will give this house away."

"Sorry, you are right."

I put my game face on and headed back out into the mean streets. Inside the glow remained.

When I returned to base, I pondered those events, and I thought about the way that family viewed Americans. The Kurds were a despised minority in their own country. We were their heroes. Their saviors. They looked at us as if we walked on water. Because of us, this family was willing to risk their lives to give us information. They understood the sacrifice that we Americans were making for them. They saw the carnage we faced every day. They were thankful.

Then my thoughts turned a corner. When was the last time I looked at Jesus as if He walked on water? My life can grow to be so burdensome that Jesus becomes "Buddy Christ."[3] He becomes my good pal who hangs out with me, but not really an Almighty Master worthy of worship. He becomes the PC God who doesn't offend anyone, who doesn't demand holiness or righteousness.

It was this attitude for which the resurrected Jesus hammered the church at Ephesus. This church had persevered through hardship and persecution. "Yet I hold this against you:

You have forsaken your first love. Remember the height from which you have fallen! Repent and do the things you did at first" (Revelation 2:4–5).

The awe of God was gone. The clutching at His clothes; the asking a million questions just to hear Jesus speak; the longing to linger in His presence. All the vivid color and life of their prior love for God had faded to gray. The Ephesian believers were still going through the motions, doing good ministry things. But their hearts lived somewhere else, loved something else.

The solution? *Repent.* That word literally means "change the mind." They needed a whole new attitude toward Christ, the Hero.

I can hear Jesus telling me the same thing. "Ministry is good, but it's not your first love. You are important and valuable, but you can't be your own first love. I'm your first love. Set your heart on Me. Take everything else off the pedestal. Worship Me as you did the day you first met Me. Remember? You couldn't get enough. Meet Me in My Word every day. Talk to Me continually. I'm here. And I will always love you."

While He was on earth, Jesus once described people like I have been: "These people honor me with their lips, but their hearts are far from me" (Matthew 15:8). That kind of conviction makes me stop and reevaluate my life, my priorities, my first love.

So many distractions can steal our hearts away from our first love. What will it take to get your attention and devotion back where it ought to be?

What idols—even good things—are keeping you from spending time with the One who sacrificed it all for you? When was the last time you looked upon the Savior and just lingered there, grabbing hold of His garment, touching His hands? Has ministry become larger than love? Has work become more of a priority than prayer? What do you need to do to reclaim your first love?

Parade of the Candy Bar

JANUARY 28, 2005

The week before the Iraqi national election, I took my entourage—a tank, a Bradley, and two Humvees—onto the streets of Khalidiyah. I took my psychological operations team with me, and through loudspeakers we proclaimed that the right to vote was open to all Iraqis. As we progressed down the crowded back streets, I told some of my infantrymen to dismount and to walk ahead of the Humvees. People emerged from their shops, from their homes, from their workplaces to see my mini-parade.

At first I held my weapon at the ready, ready to put two well-aimed shots in the chest of any insurgent who decided to peer around the corner with an RPG. I was surprised to note that the adults did not have scowls on their faces. They smiled and waved. I relaxed. In response to the Iraqis' goodwill, I ordered my men to enter a shop and buy something to show our good intentions while the loudspeakers proclaimed freedom.

I've already mentioned that the American soldier loves kids. A couple of soldiers bought a box of candy bars and started handing them out to the neighborhood children. Kids came out of the woodwork, screaming with excitement. They were practically running into the track of my tank to get candy. At first their parents looked on with smiles, then with mild concern as their children joyfully danced within inches of my lumbering seventy-two-ton tank.

I love the innocence of children. The purity of their hearts. In that moment they were not on anyone's side; there were no sides. They were not worried that an insurgent might see them taking candy from a U.S. soldier. They loved being in the moment. No disenchanting history.

These kids thought we were the greatest thing since sliced bread. That is, until we ran out of candy bars. Then disenchantment ruled. No candy, no love. Bye-bye.

As I watched them disappear, John 6 came to mind. Jesus had just fed five thousand men, plus thousands more women and children who accompanied them. When Jesus departed across the Sea of Galilee, the crowd came after Him. They hopped in boats, rafts, Jet Skis, Wave Runners to follow. Then when they found Him, Jesus did not give them more of the same. He knew they were after physical food. He knew that they needed spiritual food. So Jesus said something that sounded very strange. In fact, it sounded downright gross. "I

am the bread of heaven. If you eat of my body you will never go hungry and if you drink of my blood you shall never thirst" (my paraphrase from v. 35).

Now all of those who heard were immediately turned off. This teaching was too hard for them. The grumbling crowd dispersed, and soon only the disciples were left. Jesus looked at them and said, "You do not want to leave too, do you?" And Peter, in a rare moment of clarity, said, "Lord, to whom shall we go? You have the words of eternal life. We believe and know that you are the Holy One of God" (vv. 67–69).

When being a Christian is the cool thing, when all economic and emotional indicators point north, it's easy to go with the crowd of Christians, scrambling to get close to Jesus. Many are looking for God-sized handouts, not a lifestyle change. But being a Christian isn't always cool or profitable in the world's terms. Sometime being a Christian can actually cost you the very things you've hung around to get, like material possessions or popularity.

This is especially challenging to those who are coasting on their parents' faith. When many Christians get into college, the Army, or the "real world," they hang up their parents' Christianity like an athlete hangs up his spikes. Some of us have never developed our own faith, have never rooted our own identity deeply in Christ.

Take away the crowd and you are left with Him. Take away the cushy Christianity and see who sticks around. Too many of us are living our Christian lives in search of the next spiritual high or the next big event. When the music fades, when the reality of life sets in and the crowd is dispersing, it all comes down to you and Jesus. That's when He looks you in the eye and asks, "You do not want to leave too, do you?"

When that happens, will you be like the Iraqi children who stay only as long as the candy lasts? Or will you be like Peter who, when he sees all walking away at Christ's words, remains unfazed and says without hesitation, "You have the words of eternal life"?

Are you here just to get? Or are you willing to give your life back to the One who gave His life for you? Are you doing the Christian thing for a season, while it is cool? Or are you a lifer?

Playing Hurt

Two days before the Iraqi national elections were to begin, I prepared for the battlefield on the streets of Khalidiyah. I dismounted my tank to patrol our area on foot while my tank and a Bradley watched in the distance. We checked the Iraqi National Guard headquarters. All was well there; no signs of any movement coming from that area. One of their buildings had been blown up by insurgents the day before. Four soldiers were abducted, along with nine AK-47s and two fully automatic machine guns.

Thus our caution. I backtracked to where my men were setting up wire. Surveying their work required me to wear night-vision goggles (NVGs). If you have never worn them, they are amazing. But they give you tunnel vision.

Suddenly I was falling! My shoulder hit something hard and popped out of its socket, sending waves of pain throughout my nervous system. I wanted to scream, but was able limit my reaction to a hushed whimper instead. My NVGs switched off, so I became completely blinded. And I was stuck. My feet were unable to touch ground. I couldn't move. My shoulder started to throb.

No one had noticed that I had fallen. So I stage-whispered, "Little help here. Hey, little help!" Soon I felt several arms wrapping themselves around my flak vest.

"Watch the shoulder," I cautioned. "Watch the shoulder… easy…easy."

I was quickly pulled out of an uncovered manhole that provided access to a sewer. The bottom was twenty feet below. Only my bulky gear saved me from falling any further than I did. It may have saved my life.

Pain jerked my attention to my shoulder. Agonizing jolts rushed through my body. I knew I had to move the ball of the shoulder back into its socket.

"I got it. I got it," I said, trying to convince myself. I flexed my back slightly and then rolled my shoulder forward. There was an explosion of pain, and I felt the joint pop back into its proper place and align with the rest of my shoulder. Only then could I relax.

After a moment of self-pity, I gathered my thoughts, put my NVGs back on, and continued to survey my men's work. I determined that they were on the right track and that I did not need to watch every move they were making. Some attention from a medic sounded like a very good idea.

The medics were good to me and told me to lay off of the shoulder for a while. They advised me to have it X-rayed to make sure the scapula was not broken.

Today, I went in for the X-rays, which turned out to be inconclusive. The doctors said that I needed to rest my shoulder for a week or two to ensure that it would heal properly.

But as I write, elections are tomorrow. If you think for a

second that I'm going to let an injury take me out of the game, you're crazy.

Lots of great men of the past played while injured. They toughed it out because people depended on them. Jesus did that. The movie *The Passion of the Christ* vividly portrayed the epitome of "playing hurt." As I watched a man in that much pain rise up and take it, I could almost hear a mantra playing in the back of my mind.

I will never quit, I will never run. I will never stop till the mission's done.

I heard it as the Jews falsely accused Him.

I will never quit, I will never run. I will never stop till the mission's done.

I heard it as Peter denied Him.

I will never quit, I will never run. I will never stop till the mission's done.

I heard it as Jesus was tortured and staggered toward Calvary.

Jesus played injured.

The Old Testament prophet Isaiah wrote about the Messiah: "He was pierced for our transgressions, he was crushed for our iniquities; the punishment that brought us peace was upon him, and by his wounds we are healed. We all, like sheep, have gone astray, each of us has turned his own way; and the Lord has laid on him the iniquity of us all. He was oppressed and afflicted, yet he did not open his mouth" (Isaiah 53:5).

Jesus played injured.

Everything in Him wanted to quit. Luke records that Jesus asked the Father three times to let Him abort the mission (see Luke 22:39–46). Each time the answer was no. There was no turning back. Jesus chose obediently to do what He came to do.

Sometimes in life we are emotionally or spiritually wounded, and we feel like quitting. We make excuses why we can't do what we know we should. *It's too hard to stick with this job. I can't stand this marriage for another second.* Maybe it's a church that hurt you too badly, and you can't go back. Maybe a friend has wounded you, and you can't trust anyone anymore.

I don't know the issue, but I know that Jesus played hurt, so that we could, too.

Jesus doesn't expect us to endure Calvary; only He could do that. But He says, "I am with you always, even to the end of the earth" (my paraphrase of Matthew 28:20). Whatever you're facing, His presence and power will help you through it. If you're willing to obey. If you'll choose to play hurt.

Are you ready to quit because you are hurt?
What pain do you need to share with God?
With someone else who cares? Maybe you need
a break. How can you strategically prepare now
for a lifelong commitment to God's mission?

I will never quit, I will never run.
I will never stop till the mission's done.

Christ didn't quit. Christ is in you.
Stay the course.

Freedom in Iraq

JANUARY 31, 2005

Euphoria has broken out across Iraq. And not just with the nationals; I'm caught up in it, too. Yesterday was an incredible day. Election Day—January 30, 2005—has gone down in history as a victory for the free world, and a defeat for terrorists in their holes. We were prepared for the day. We had extra security at every voting site. Every tank and Bradley available was in sector, poised and ready to pounce on any terrorist who would dare to disrupt freedom's charge.

We were able to foil the terrorists. They placed a bomb in a building. We found it. Then they tried to slip an antitank mine on the road. We found it. Wherever a terrorist popped up, we stopped him. Nothing was going to prevent this election from succeeding. For the first time in almost fifty years, Iraqis would actually get to choose their leaders.

Our area was secure, but we knew we were still in Sunni Iraq. The Sunni leaders had urged their followers to boycott the elections out of disdain for the American forces who conducted them. These leaders thought their political impact would sway the rest of Iraq.

They were wrong. Record numbers of voters turned out. More than eight million Iraqis entered the polls. That's more than half the country's people—a better turnout than in any Western country, where we've grown apathetic about our freedom.

That overwhelming victory is apparent now. But early on Election Day it was far from obvious. In our Sunni-entrenched area of operations, the now-open polls sat empty. Everyone held back. It seemed that no one would vote. Until an old woman, wearing the traditional black abaya and tennis shoes, walked up to the metal detector. She valiantly went forward. The entire community watched from a distance. She slipped into the building. Fifteen minutes later, out she walked, her right hand raised, her index finger extended. Purple indelible ink stained her finger, showing that she had voted.

"I vote! I vote!" she exclaimed in a thick Arabic accent. Then she defiantly left the polling station and went home. Streams of people began to flow through the metal detector to play their part in changing history. So much for projections of zero turnout.

Today I spoke with my interpreter, Mohammed. He had talked to his father on the phone. He spoke with contagious excitement, his Arab-accented English especially thick. "Suhr, Suhr!" he exclaimed. "Suhr, my father! He tell me, he tell me about the elections. He say that many peoples in line. My entire family vote. My grandmother, who is eighty-eight years old. She vote! This amazing time in Iraq." He stopped for a moment. His eyes had a glassy glint. "We have freedom!"

I looked away, not wanting anyone to see the tears building in my own eyes. This was beautiful. All we had sacrificed here was for this day. The two soldiers my company lost. The eleven soldiers that my battalion lost. The more than two thousand Coalition forces killed rescuing a people from an evil regime, giving Iraqis freedom.

God considered His sacrifice worth it too. He rescued us. Gave us freedom. Colossians 1:13 says, "For [God] has rescued us from the dominion of darkness and brought us into the kingdom of the Son he loves."

Paul, writing to the Galatians, opens his letter like this: "Grace and peace to you from God our Father and the Lord Jesus Christ, who gave himself for our sins to rescue us from the present evil age" (1:3–4).

Americans and other Coalition forces sacrificed their young men and women for the liberation of Iraq. God sacrificed His Son for the liberation of your soul.

Today signaled Iraq's first real freedom in a long time. There had been so-called "elections" before, but this time the people had a voice that made a difference. This time the masses weren't just used to rubberstamp Saddam's power ploys.

Today there was much rejoicing. Today there was victory. Today was a new page in the history of Iraq.

I hope your life story resounds with an even greater celebration.

Have you experienced the freedom that Christ bought for you with His life? If not, are you afraid to admit or let go of your sin? Are you trying to pay for your own freedom by being good enough? If you have freedom in Christ, do you regularly celebrate it? Have you shared your freedom with someone else?

There is only one way to experience true freedom. Receive as a gift the sacrifice of Jesus Christ in your place. He accepts you no matter what you've done. He forgives completely. And you can't free yourself.

The Road Ahead

The elections are over. Finally the land will find peace. Or so I thought.

About a week after the elections, the euphoria has been shattered. The insurgents are back at it again. Yesterday was rough. It started out with an antitank mine that destroyed a Humvee. Thank God, no one was injured. But the Humvee was totaled.

I was surprised by the attack and wanted to believe that the antitank mine must have been put there before the elections, before peace had settled in the land. It must be an anomaly.

I was wrong.

"Apache Tango, this is White 2. My loader has been shot! Sniper fire!"

"White 2, White 2, what is the status of the casualty?"

"I am bringing him in."

That was all I needed. I pointed at my quick reaction force. Without hesitation, they sprinted for our vehicles. I started putting on my gear.

"Give me a SITREP!" I demanded.

"Sir, White 2 has been shot. White 1 is moving to his location to try and find the sniper. White 2 is moving to the West Gate to meet Apache Band-Aid! He was shot in the hand."

"Roger."

Here we go again, I thought as I grabbed my M4 rifle and moved down the stairs to my tank. It was already powered up and ready to go.

"Sir, the radios are filled and on. We have gotten radio checks with Tango. We are ready when you are," my loader said, his eyes focused on me, ready for my command as I got on the tank.

I got a thumbs-up from my wingman, and we were off. We quickly moved to the vicinity of the sniper. I had my infantry on the ground, going through houses, looking for signs of the enemy. Nothing.

"Apache 6! Apache 6! This is Reaper 1. I just had an RPG fired at me!"

"Roger, give me your location. I am moving time: now!"

I told my infantry to wrap it up there. We had to respond to other action. My entourage, consisting of my tank, a Bradley, and two Humvees, made its way to Reaper 1—our code name for LT Kelly Sanders—and started scouring the area. Reaper 1 had destroyed a small building, from which the enemy had fired an RPG. I pulled in by the building, dismounted, and started patrolling with my infantry squad. We found the round casing from the RPG and went to search the nearest house.

We ended up detaining three men for further questioning, leaving the women beating their breasts and pulling out their hair. I sighed and remounted my tank. For public safety, I used my tank to completely flatten the damaged building.

As I drove back to base, I realized I was frustrated. It seemed that the elections changed nothing and that this insanity would go on forever. However, as I thought about it, I realized that democracy was a process. It would take time for these people to let go of their old ways and embrace freedom.

I thought of myself. I still struggle to embrace freedom. I still fight daily with my insurgent flesh that tries to deny me the freedom which comes with a righteous and holy life. I tend to move toward the things that bind me up and leave my heart weak and longing. I am just like this Iraqi country. I am free, but every day I am fighting to overcome my own weaknesses. As I look to the future of Iraq, I see a bright democracy ahead. It will take time. The people have to learn a completely new way of life.

The newly established church at Colossi faced a similar struggle. The believers had joyously received freedom through faith in Christ. But then began a spiritual civil war within each liberated man and woman, the old habits fighting to take back the reigns on each life. That's why Paul wrote to the Colossians,

"Since, then, you have been raised with Christ…put to death… whatever belongs to your earthly nature: sexual immorality, impurity, lust, evil desires and greed, which is idolatry" (3:1, 5).

Some Christians believe that victory over the old regime is an automatic thing. *Once you accept Christ, you don't have to worry about this stuff,* they think. But if this were so, Paul would not have needed to instruct us to actively resist sin. Yet that's exactly the challenge we face.

What is more, not only did Paul instruct us to put to death our old way of living, but also to learn a new way. "As God's chosen people, holy and dearly loved, clothe yourselves with compassion, kindness, humility, gentleness and patience" (v. 12). Paul says to take something off and get rid of it; he also says to put something else on.

The complete wardrobe change is a vast undertaking, and it can't happen overnight. Thankfully, God offers us a paradoxical solution. We can't be perfect immediately, but He accepts us as we are, at every stage of our transformation. And although we lack the ability to effect this transformation on our own, Christ's power works in us, daily taking us one step closer to the full realization of our freedom (see 1:29). I love that. I can't do it by myself. I must let Christ work through me with His energy to accomplish that which only He can.

Iraq has accepted democracy, but still faces insurgents who fight against freedom at every turn. If you've received Christ as Savior, you've accepted freedom. It's real, and it's yours now. But your old ways will continue to drag you down until you let Christ penetrate your very core. Then God's infinite power can work its miracle in you.

Are you frustrated because sin keeps nipping at your heels? Does your life resemble more of the old person before Christ than the new one? Are you willing to invite Christ to work in you with His divine power? Are you committed to actively cooperating, making hard choices to put off the old and put on the new? What will you do today?

Put Your Money Where Your Mouth Is

FEBRUARY 10, 2005

God is so good! Here I am in Iraq, and I have just received a ridiculous amount of stuff from people in the United States. This is crazy. A ministry in Atlanta called "7:22," led by Louie Giglio, just sent us about six thousand bucks' worth of DVDs and players, CDs and players, MP3 players, video games, books, Gatorade, sheets, toothbrushes, and toothpaste. I think we have enough toothpaste here to prevent cavities for the next generation and enough video games to satisfy our soldiers' addictions for a lifetime. It's overwhelming. God's goodness through these generous people is too much to comprehend. And this isn't the first. Less than a year ago, Louie and his ministry donated $1,500 worth of DVDs, CDs, and books. How unbelievable is that?

I am not going to compare salaries here, but I will tell you that with just that donation, God has provided me much more than I have given Him in my offerings to Him. Since I have been over here, I have received, in gifts for my soldiers, about five times the amount I have given God.

Proverbs 3:9–10 comes to mind: "Honor the LORD with your wealth, with the firstfruits of all your crops; then your barns will be filled to overflowing, and your vats will brim over with new wine." I've honestly tried to express my gratitude to God by giving Him from my wealth. And He has poured back even more.

Sometimes we distrust God's ability to provide for us, so we protect our money. In fact, we protect it from Him! All in the name of "good management," of course.

At the end of the Old Testament, God issues an amazing challenge concerning this problem. "Bring the whole tithe into the storehouse [of the temple, Israel's place of worship], that there may be food in my house. Test me in this...and see if I will not throw open the floodgates of heaven and pour out so much blessing that you will not have room enough for it" (Malachi 3:10).

This is the only place in the Bible where God says, "Test me." I did a double take when I read this, because I was a lot more familiar with the statements of Jesus when He was dueling with the devil in the desert (see Matthew 4:1-11). At that time, He quoted from Deuteronomy 6:16: "Do not test the LORD your God."

But apparently God has made one exception to this rule. Here, God is challenging Israel to show their faith by the way they allocate their treasure. The "tithe" He mentions means "one tenth." It was a guideline to help the people understand the kind of generosity that would honor God. It's not intended as a legalistic formula, but as a beginning point for even greater generosity.

In any case, God clearly promises that He will provide abundantly when you give with an open heart. You give to God, and God gives you an overflow.

I never expected this principle to be so dramatically evidenced here in Iraq. It just happened. It's God doing His thing. If we know God and His Word, this should not shock us. But throughout history and today in our materialistic world, we have fallen into the habit of grasping our wealth with clenched fists, and we haven't allowed God to respond to generosity from His bottomless cornucopia. We know nothing but self-protection of self-interests, and the resulting meager return.

Jesus said, "Where your treasure is, there your heart will be also" (Luke 12:34; Matthew 6:21). If your money goes to heavenly things, then your heart will indeed follow it. That is why our giving is important to *God*. It is not as though God needs our money. This is God we are talking about.

Why does He want your treasure? Because He know that's where your heart is! And what does God want? Not your money, but your heart! He wants you.

Hebrews 11:1 says, "Faith is being sure of what we hope for, and certain of what we do not see." I hear a lot about Christians going all over the world to preach the gospel. I hear of zealous Christian friends winning souls to Christ. We talk a lot about having faith. But less than 10 percent of those who call themselves "born again" give 10 percent or more of what God has given them. I guess God can save our soul, but we can't trust Him with our 401K.

You don't give to God for salvation. You don't give to God for His acceptance and love. You give money to God in order to give Him your heart and to show Him your faith. Giving is an expression of love and trust.

Are you lavish with God's love, but Scrooge-like with your money? Are you afraid to test God with your money?

Think about the present and future eternal blessings you're missing because you're holding on to the temporary treasures of this world.

Put your money where you mouth is.

Soccer Balls Anyone?

Virginia Cook Realtors of Dallas, Texas, has made a habit of spoiling my men. Their latest operation was to send one hundred fifty soccer balls for my men to give to the Iraqis. Equipped with these gifts, we can share the love of the United States with the Iraqi people and build new bonds with them.

In addition, First Baptist Church of Dallas, Georgia, donated about two hundred Beanie Babies and dolls to help us befriend the children.

My men spent a couple days blowing up the soccer balls, and then we started taking all of the gifts into sector. We went to the Kurdish district. This is an area where the people are generally friendly to us, but the Sunni terrorists like to fire at us because when we fire back, there is a greater chance of damage to Kurdish people and property. We chose a particular intersection where we were fired upon most frequently and where the IED attacks were the most intense. Terrorists also bombed two Iraqi police buildings and an Iraqi National Guard building in this area, destroying millions of dollars of property and killing many Iraqis. I decided right there would be the perfect spot to give away soccer balls and Beanies.

"Keep your eyes peeled, boys," I radioed to the Bradley and two Humvees that were traveling with my tank. I assigned the Humvees to watch the roads that entered the area, and I put the tank and Bradley just off center at the intersection. As soon as the kids saw us giving away a soccer ball, they came running!

It was awesome. Soon the entire intersection was flooded with kids. They were falling all over themselves to get a chance at a gift.

One little boy ran up to me and said, "I am a Christian! Do you love Jesus?" I got so excited. He was the first Christian that I met on the streets of Khalidiyah. Then he said, "Give me football!" I was delighted to oblige his request.

I was having a great time. I had kids trying to tackle me and rip soccer balls from my hands. I felt like a varsity football player breaking through a line of Pee-Wees. We spent about an hour mingling with the kids, listening to their requests for pens and pencils and more soccer balls. We handed out some candy and enjoyed the swarm of little bodies.

I hopped on the tank to grab some more Beanie Babies when my gunner abruptly said, "Sir, we gotta go."

I looked up, and sure enough, the kids had started to clear out. Bad sign. I didn't hesitate. "Let's go! Let's go! Let's go!"

My men immediately switched hats. (Actually, "helmets" would be a more fitting metaphor.) They changed over from humanitarian to warrior. With grace and determination they readied their weapons and returned to their vehicles. I noticed a man shooing some of the kids away. I wasn't sure if he was Mujahadin or just a concerned father gathering up the kids.

Potential sniper positions were everywhere amongst building rooftops; the enemy had his choice of firing angles from all 360 degrees. I wasn't about to stay and find out what he had planned. All I know is that when a battle comes, I want to be the attacker.

As I left the area and headed back to base, I thought about the reason why I got out of there so quickly. It just didn't feel right. I knew something was amiss. I couldn't ignore the warning signs.

So many times, we find ourselves in spiritual danger. We may be in a situation fraught with temptation, but we ignore the nagging heart conviction and the telltale danger signs. Instead of making a wise choice, we do what feels good. We give in to warped logic. *There's nothing wrong with going to his apartment. One little drink won't hurt. Is anyone really going to get upset if I tell a half-truth? I know she's married, but we both have to eat dinner, right? Why not together?*

In Matthew 10:16, Jesus said, "I am sending you out like sheep among wolves. Therefore be as shrewd as snakes and as innocent as doves."

The Christian life is not easy. Even while doing good and harmless things, we face potential temptations. A well-intentioned woman tries to lead a guy to Christ and ends up in a compromising situation. A well-intentioned man tries to offer godly counsel, alone, to a woman in a troubled marriage. Then one thing leads to another...

Paul assures us, "No temptation has seized you except what is common to man. And God is faithful; he will not let you be tempted beyond what you can bear. But when you are tempted, he will also provide a way out so that you can stand up under it" (1 Corinthians 10:13). Take a step back. Take a deep breath. Look for the exit. God will show it to you.

The exit strategy may require you to conduct a humbling spiritual inventory. You may need to admit weaknesses and imperfections. But your humility allows Christ's strength to come to your rescue and protect you.

Earlier in this book I introduced David's prayer in Psalm 139:23–24. When you're in a spiritually dangerous situation, that's another great time to pray, "Search me, O God, and know my heart; test me and know my anxious thoughts. See if there is any offensive way in me, and lead me in the way everlasting."

It may be painful to listen honestly to God's response, but if you are serious about conquering sin, His surgical intervention is essential.

Be astutely shrewd—shrewd as a serpent—as you examine yourself. Be vulnerably innocent—innocent as a dove—as you open yourself to God.

And when you detect signs of attack, *run!*

What potential ambushes do you regularly walk into? How could your "innocent" situations turn deadly? Will you ask God to search your heart? Will you listen to His diagnosis?

Be shrewd. Be innocent.

His Ways Are Not My Ways

The other night a friend of mine, Captain Craig Evans, called me on the radio. "Apache 6, this is Currahee 3A. Are you in your command post?"

"Roger," I responded.

"Okay. Well, I need to talk to you."

I wondered what could be so important that he would come to me? No one ventures down to my Tactical Operations Center (TOC) without good reason. I waited nervously, shuffling papers and trying to clean up. But my mind was distracted, wondering what could be so important that Craig would need to actually come visit me at this late hour.

He walked into the TOC with a solemn face, and I knew something was wrong. I started recounting everything recently that I could have done wrong, but was drawing blanks.

"What's up, Craig?" I asked.

"I have some bad news. Your friend Captain Gade…Dan… he got hit by an IED."

My heart sank.

He continued, "He is in the hospital, and there is about a fifty-fifty chance he will make it."

I was stunned. This is my buddy Dan. He is the other tank company commander out here in the Wild West. When it comes to tanks, it is me and then Dan. That's it. Dan was two years ahead of me at West Point. We were friends at West

Point in Officer Christian Fellowship, and then we were friends as we served in 2-72 Armor together in Korea. I looked up to Dan. Dan was the invincible guy. No one could touch him on physical fitness tests, and no one was smarter than him. He loved Jesus and was born again. He could run circles around anyone tactically, and he could out-reason anyone. He had an indomitable spirit.

And now he might die?

I started praying. *Lord, what are you doing here? Are you taking Dan?* I tried to make sense of it. To understand how this all fit into the big plan. Dan was going to Syracuse to get his master's degree, and then he was going to teach at West Point.

He has a gorgeous wife, Wendy, and a beautiful three-year-old daughter, Anna Grace. And this makes sense how?

It just so happens that I was reading through the book of Isaiah, and I came across Isaiah 55:8–9, where God says, "My thoughts are not your thoughts, neither are your ways my ways.… As the heavens are higher than the earth, so are my ways higher than your ways and my thoughts than your thoughts."

These words pierce my heart. I can't begin to fathom how God is working this out. In the end, all of this will be for God's renown. I cannot bend God's plan to make it fit into mine; I must mold myself into His. I don't understand, but I know He has a plan.

Romans 8:26–28 also helped me in my confusion. "In the same way, the Spirit helps us in our weakness. We do not know what we ought to pray for, but the Spirit himself intercedes for us with groans that words cannot express. And he who searches our hearts knows the mind of the Spirit, because the Spirit intercedes for the saints in accordance with God's will. And we know that in all things God works for the good of those who love him, who have been called according to His purpose."

I am not sure what to pray. I don't know how Dan is doing right now as he lays in a hospital in Germany fighting for his life. What I do know is that God knows what I should pray, so I lift up my groan to God. I let Him search my heart and I ask Him to help me conform to His will. I have to trust that God doesn't make empty promises. I have to believe He knows what He is doing. For the God who allowed Dan to get hit by an IED and endure suffering is the same God who put His own Son on the cross.

What are you going through that makes no sense to you? How are you questioning the way God is carrying out business? Will you let God conform your will to His? Will you pray, even if you can't find the words?

Remember: No matter what...God is still on the throne.

Editor's note: Dan survived, but had to have his right leg amputated. After numerous surgeries and work with prosthetics, Dan is now walking and leading a happy and healthy life with his wife and daughter.

Who Will Win the Day?

FEBRUARY 17, 2005

The dawn blazes a hue of orange and blue
And it seems that there is so much to do
The question rises in my mind
How much longer? How much more time?
When will freedom reign across this land?
What is in store? What is His plan?
The restless spirit within
Wants it now.
Wants freedom to reign, insurgents to die
Fact I cannot deny
But there is so much pain
And so much profane
I wonder.

The cool air bites my skin
I climb aboard my tank and go again
RPGs, mortars, and sniper fire
The same as the day prior
I thought freedom had dawned its cloak
And the heart of the insurgent would grow remote
"Move out!" I call to the driver of my beast
We drive toward the fire which has yet to cease
Engaging the enemy with all we have
There seems little cause to smile or laugh
I pause.
In my heart as the battle rages
I feel history starting to turn its pages
Freedom comes at a price.

I am tired and want to sleep
Rest is what I seek
It seems just as I am about to fall
I hear another call
The battle rages once again
Bringing my slumber to an end
And I rise to answer the sound
Upon my heart it seems to pound

Relentless in our fight
Is what we must be
And stand to face the enemy
When freedom's call is challenged at heart
Never forget the reason for this start.

I can hear the drumbeat playing
I can see them watching on
I can hear their muffled voices
Calling us to keep driving on
I press toward the enemy
Whom I cannot see
I press toward the enemy
Who is always watching me
I have more weapons at my disposal
Than the enemy could ever fathom.

The trap is set
On that you can bet
My confidence is my demise
Only the discerning and wise
Can see the way to victory
Vigilance
Consistency
Takes away the heart
Of the enemy.
The roar of my tank under my feet
Is sure to bring the enemy to defeat
I have the power and understand my place
Lead my men to stand and face
Whatever may lie ahead
Not to avenge my dead
But to preserve the way ahead
So that the future may tread
Upon what is now a battleground
But later transformed.
A place where hope was torn
Where hope has become forlorn
To a place where we no longer mourn.

We bow our heads to pray.
Only You, Lord, can win the day.

Notes

1. ∞ is the mathematical symbol for "infinity."
2. Thanks to Louie Giglio for this phrase.
3. This is a name I got from the movie *Dogma*.

Mrs. Nina Mascheck